D0368912

Additional Praise for
The Warren Buffetts Next Door

"How real people make real money from stocks. Forget the Wall Street hype, read this!"

—Clem Chambers, CEO ADVFN.com, Investorshub.com;
Author of *The Armageddon Trade* and *The Twain Maxim*

"Matt Schifrin has written an informative book, demonstrating a few of the many paths to investing success. In investing, as in many of life's endeavors, passion, hard work, and discipline can outweigh theory and education."

—Ron Muhlenkamp, Founder and President,
Muhlenkamp & Company; Author of *Ron's Road to Wealth*

The
Warren Buffetts
Next Door

The Warren Buffetts Next Door

THE WORLD'S GREATEST INVESTORS YOU'VE NEVER HEARD OF AND WHAT YOU CAN LEARN FROM THEM

Matthew Schifrin,
Forbes

WILEY

John Wiley & Sons, Inc.

Copyright © 2011 by Forbes LLC and Matthew Schifrin. All rights reserved.

Published by John Wiley & Sons, Inc., Hoboken, New Jersey.
Published simultaneously in Canada.

No part of this publication may be reproduced, stored in a retrieval system, or transmitted in any form or by any means, electronic, mechanical, photocopying, recording, scanning, or otherwise, except as permitted under Section 107 or 108 of the 1976 United States Copyright Act, without either the prior written permission of the Publisher, or authorization through payment of the appropriate per-copy fee to the Copyright Clearance Center, Inc., 222 Rosewood Drive, Danvers, MA 01923, (978) 750-8400, fax (978) 646-8600, or on the Web at www.copyright.com. Requests to the Publisher for permission should be addressed to the Permissions Department, John Wiley & Sons, Inc., 111 River Street, Hoboken, NJ 07030, (201) 748-6011, fax (201) 748-6008, or online at http://www.wiley.com/go/permissions.

Limit of Liability/Disclaimer of Warranty: While the publisher and author have used their best efforts in preparing this book, they make no representations or warranties with respect to the accuracy or completeness of the contents of this book and specifically disclaim any implied warranties of merchantability or fitness for a particular purpose. No warranty may be created or extended by sales representatives or written sales materials. The advice and strategies contained herein may not be suitable for your situation. You should consult with a professional where appropriate. Neither the publisher nor author shall be liable for any loss of profit or any other commercial damages, including but not limited to special, incidental, consequential, or other damages.

For general information on our other products and services or for technical support, please contact our Customer Care Department within the United States at (800) 762-2974, outside the United States at (317) 572-3993 or fax (317) 572-4002.

Wiley also publishes its books in a variety of electronic formats. Some content that appears in print may not be available in electronic books. For more information about Wiley products, visit our web site at www.wiley.com.

Forbes is a registered trademark of Forbes LLC. Its use is pursuant to a license agreement.

Library of Congress Cataloging-in-Publication Data:
Schifrin, Matthew.
    The Warren Buffetts next door : the world's greatest investors you've never heard of and what you can learn from them / Matthew Schifrin.
        p. cm.
    Includes index.
    ISBN 978-0-470-57378-5 (hardback); 978-0-470-91530-1 (ebk); 978-0-470-91529-5 (ebk)
    1. Investments.   2. Investment analysis.   3. Electronic trading of securities.   I. Title.
    HG4521.S35142 2010
    332.6—dc22

                                                                    2010021343
Printed in the United States of America

10   9   8   7   6   5   4   3   2   1

To my mother Marcella,
whose warmth left us too soon,
and my father, Marvin,
who taught me to question everything.

To Susan, Noah, and Elisabeth,
who light up my life.

Contents

Foreword

Matt Schifrin has written one of the most unusual—and useful—investment books you will ever find. Instead of trotting out some supposedly surefire formula on how to get rich, Matt has chronicled the successes of 10 individuals you have never heard of. He gives you unvarnished investment insights from people who mastered this arena *on their own*. Precisely because they are self-taught, their stories should have particular relevance—and inspiration—for millions of do-it-yourself investors.

Several things pop out immediately:

- There is *no one way* to achieve success. Each of these people has developed his own particular approach.
- They do share two characteristics: hard work and iron discipline. They don't rely on tips from TV talking heads, friends, or acquaintances. They spend hours digging, and digging hard. They use the Web. While they take in reams of information from the Web and elsewhere, they make up their own minds.

Everyone likes to think he or she is disciplined. But most investors give in to their emotions when the market seems to be rising relentlessly or plunging sickeningly.

- These next-door Buffetts make mistakes—but they actually learn from them.
- Every one of them has suffered a searing market setback. Even investor John Navin, who had successfully avoided devastating losses during the 2008 and early 2009 market meltdown, missed the subsequent market upsurge.

Another thing that comes across loud and clear is the extraordinary phenomenon of the Web. It is truly empowering and liberating for individuals who didn't go to prestigious business schools or take formal courses in finance and security analysis. At the end of the book, Matt helpfully gives readers his take on web sites that do-it-yourself individuals can employ.

But most of these investors are employing the Web not just for facts, figures, ratings, and lists, but also for interacting with other individuals. In other words, the Internet allows constant brainstorming. You may be alone at your keyboard, but in terms of give-and-take, you could literally be at a stadium filled with other interested individuals.

What also becomes clear here is how the Web allows individuals, regardless of their circumstances, to develop talents that otherwise would have lain dormant. But while the Web is a great opportunity creator, it is no guarantor of success. It is a tool—a profoundly helpful one—but it is a means to an end.

Thus, the book both inspires and cautions. As always, there are no quick, easy roads to riches. But now people have unprecedented opportunities to create meaningful wealth over time—if they have stick-to-itiveness and the maturity to know there will be plenty of bumps along the way.

—Steve Forbes

Acknowledgments

I would like to thank all the people who contributed to this book in many ways.

First and foremost I would like to thank Steve and Tim Forbes for encouraging my entrepreneurism as an editor. I also owe a great deal of thanks to my mentor and former editor, the late Jim Michaels. He set the bar high for *Forbes* reporters and inspired a generation of great financial journalists.

This book would not have been possible without a great deal of help from Ken Kam and his team at Marketocracy. Similar thanks are due to Adam Menzel and the crew at Ticker Technologies. I would also like to thank Barbara Strauch and my brother Andrew Schifrin for helping to get this project started. Thanks is also due to my friend Jason Zweig for helping me come up with the book's name. I am also grateful for the support I got from Laura Walsh and Judy Howarth at John Wiley & Sons.

I would especially like to thank Tina Russo McCarthy, one of the unsung heroes at *Forbes*, who spent tireless hours in her spare time discussing this book with me and making sure that all of my i's were dotted and t's crossed.

Last but not least, I would like to thank my family, Susan, Noah, and Elisabeth, for putting things on hold while I worked on this book, and for being a great sounding board for my ideas.

INTRODUCTION

Thou Shalt Covet Thy Neighbor's Portfolio

In February 2000, at the peak of the bubble in dot-com stocks, I wrote a story in a special edition of *Forbes* magazine that had a provocative blurb on the cover posing the question: "Will the Web Produce the Next Warren Buffett?"

The article chronicled several amateur investors who were riding high during that raging bull market. One of them was a 47-year-old housewife who lived on a cattle ranch in Nebraska. After seeing her family nest egg languish in the high fee mutual funds that her broker had sold her, she went online to a site called ClearStation.com and taught herself about price-earnings multiples and moving averages. Another success story was a schoolteacher from Wisconsin, and yet another was a Vietnamese immigrant who worked for the phone company by day but trolled sites like Yahoo and Briefing.com for stock ideas at night.

A little more than a month later, the dot-com bubble burst and most of the tech stocks these amateurs had big profits in came crashing down. The party was over for these bull market heroes.

Or was it? There were five million online investors when I wrote that article. Today there are an estimated 50 million in the United States alone. I now think of the amateur online investors I profiled in February 2000 as merely an early wave in the gathering troops of self-directed investors. Today's online investors are equipped with great technology and a seemingly endless armament of information, tools, and online resources.

Some have made grand predictions of how the onslaught of self-taught investors will break down the walls protecting the mighty financial institutions that have dominated the financial landscape for a century. That investors are on a mission to free themselves from the yoke of high commissions and fees and middling advice. Could be, but I think individual investor goals are a lot less ambitious.

Self-directed investors are merely looking to improve their lot in life, to be able to afford to take a family vacation each year, to buy that lakefront house, or to send their kids to a good college. They want to ensure that they will have enough income to last them through retirement. Investors are beginning to realize that devoting time toward making your money work for you is a lot smarter than working for your money. After all, the tax code, which favors long-term capital gains and dividend income, encourages this behavior.

What is clearly changing is the notion—ingrained in our psyche for generations—that only qualified financial professionals are capable of directing our investments prudently—you know, the ones with diplomas from Wharton and Harvard who illustrate their investment strategies with polished PowerPoint presentations. "Better leave it to the professionals," is the common refrain. Unfortunately that didn't work out so well in 2008.

This book is living proof that regular people have the ability to become outstanding investors in their own right. Sitting at home with a Web-connected computer, you can now produce the kinds of investment returns most believe are only attainable at the most sophisticated and exclusive hedge funds. The 10 "Warren Buffetts Next Door" profiled in this book can pick stocks better than the vast majority of all professional financial advisors and money managers employed by firms like Merrill Lynch and Fidelity.

On February 26, 2010, the most famous investor in the world, billionaire Warren Buffett, released Berkshire Hathaway's 2009 results in his much-anticipated Chairman's letter. In the year following one of the worst stock market declines in history, mighty Berkshire's book value increased by 19.8 percent. The results were pretty good, but what really counts for shareholders is the performance of Berkshire Hathaway's New York Stock Exchange listed A-shares. In 2009, Warren only delivered a 3 percent gain on his shareholders money, and no dividends. The S&P 500 gained 27 percent.

I am not using this example to challenge the notion that Warren Buffett is the greatest investor of all time. His 45-year record and his personal net worth are proof enough for me. But I am saying that the investing intelligence that he and others like him have perfected is spreading.

About 1,350 miles away from Buffett's Omaha headquarters in the suburbs of Sacramento, California, Mike Koza, a 51-year-old civil engineer for the county department of waste management applies many of the same Graham & Dodd value principles in selecting stocks for his personal portfolio.

Since February 2001, he has been able to achieve an average annual return of 34 percent per year.[1] An investment in Berkshire's stock would have gotten you 6 percent per year. An investment in a well-run index fund like Vanguard Total Stock Market? Less than 2 percent on average per year.

Koza is not alone. Another Warren Buffett wannabe profiled in Chapter 1 named Chris Rees practices concentrated deep value investing from his ocean-view home on the balmy north coast of the Dominican Republic. His verifiable average annual return since he began being tracked online in October 2000 is 25 percent.[2]

Jack Weyland, 33, of Reno, Nevada, has developed an expertise in health care and biotech stocks. He has had an average annual return of 36 percent since July 2002. Neither he nor Rees ever completed college, and Jack Weyland has spent much of his time picking stocks while on the road driving a tractor-trailer.

But investing success is not just about returns versus an index; it is about affording a lifestyle and attaining your goals. Alan T. Hill, profiled in Chapter 5, was able to secure a golden retirement with a single smart stock pick that created a windfall allowing him to build an adobe-style dream home in Placitas, New Mexico. Alan is no flash in the pan either. Since he retired as president of an educational technology foundation in 2005, Hill, 71, is making more money investing than he ever did during his career.

All of the people profiled in this book are risk takers. But they are also supersensitive to losing their own hard-earned capital, so the investment risks they take are carefully calculated. The Warren Buffetts Next Door profiled in this book come from all walks of life, but every single one of them is smart about using the Web as both a resource for investor education and as a tool in sourcing and fleshing out stock ideas. The Web, along with rock-bottom commission schedules at e-brokers, has truly been transformative.

Online investing and all that it entails is eliminating the need to have some special advantage in life as a prerequisite for investment success. In the late 1960s it took a lucky golf caddying assignment to get Peter Lynch in the door as an intern at Fidelity Investments. Then it took Lynch nearly a decade more to acquire the skills necessary to become the portfolio manager of the Fidelity Magellan Fund.

Thousands have attended elite schools like Buffett's alma mater Columbia Business School, and others have toiled for hours in pursuit of Chartered Financial Analysts designations trying to learn to become great investors. But imagine how quickly Benjamin Graham's lessons on securities analysis would have spread in the world of Google, Twitter, and YouTube?

The excellent, but relatively unknown investors profiled in this book are just ten of thousands more armchair investors out there taking control of their own portfolio decisions. For the purposes of finding my candidates for *The Warren Buffetts Next Door,* I relied on Web-based sources for verifiable track records. Marketocracy .com, a site created in the summer of 2000 with rigorous standards for monitoring investment performance, was my number one source because its data is deepest and goes back the farthest. I consider Marketocracy.com to be an incubator of legendary investors, and you can find out more about them in Chapter 11.

I also used another Web community called ValueForum.com to find candidates for this book. I have spent hundreds of hours reviewing web sites as investing editor of *Forbes* and before that as editor of *Forbes Best of the Web.* It would be difficult for me to name a smarter, more collaborative community of self-directed investors than this small subscription web site. In fact, ValueForum has held community stock-picking contests since January 2004, and as a group its members are up 88 percent versus 16 percent for the S&P 500.[3] The men I selected from ValueForum.com are all highly rated in the online community and have proven to be outstanding long-term investors. Each is living an enviable lifestyle as a result.

Some may argue that a few of the investors profiled in this book are paper tigers because it is their virtual portfolios that are being used to judge their investment success. This is a fair point because virtual money and real money are not the same thing. Still, the virtual portfolios I cite in this book are being held to rigorous standards—in some ways more stringent than returns touted for hedge funds and other professional money managers.

For example, Marketocracy won't let its money managers execute a trade for more than 10 percent of the average daily volume of any stock. This keeps them from stuffing their portfolio with illiquid penny stocks over a short period of time (it also limits the size of any one holding to 25 percent). Marketocracy managers' performance figures are also reported after deducting commissions of $0.05 per share and management fees of 1.95 percent.

After interviewing candidates for this book, I found that in cases where the virtual managers had sufficient investment capital, they were mirroring their real-life portfolios in their virtual funds. And if Marketocracy fulfills its pledge, these paper tigers may one day brandish some real teeth. Marketocracy's asset management affiliate is currently putting real capital to work in the stocks of its best-performing virtual money managers.

When reading about each of the Warren Buffetts Next Door in this book, it is a good idea to pay attention not only to the strategy lessons, investing rules and case studies in each chapter but also the biographical information. Mike Koza, for example would not have discovered his amazing talent for picking winning stocks if not for his wife Maria, whom he met at age 40. I firmly believe that personal histories and life situations are as important to investment success as are say, clear thinking and an affinity for mathematics.

To be sure, some of the great armchair investors profiled in this book may flame out in the coming years. I will do my best to keep you updated on their investing successes and failures on Forbes.com.

However, even if some of these successful Warren-wannabes crash and burn, there will be dozens more outstanding self-taught investors to take their place. In a world where the vast majority of professional money managers fail to even perform as well as a stock market index fund, it's worth it for all of us to consider that you don't necessarily need someone else's advice to improve your financial well-being. You can learn to be a great investor, a Warren Buffett Next Door, and you don't need a lot of money or fancy equipment to do so.

Ever since the government encouraged corporate America to abolish defined benefit pension plans in favor of defined contribution or 401(k) plans, most of us have unwittingly been handed the keys to our financial future. The devastating stock market collapse of 2008 has woken us up to the fact that parking what's left of your nest egg in an index fund, or handing it over to an *expert*, may not be the best solution.

Among professional money managers, mediocrity reigns. As for financial advisors or brokers, most are much more attuned to gaining your confidence and gathering your assets than they are to choosing investments that will make your money grow.

My hope is that you will read about my 10 Warren Buffetts Next Door and realize that the only real prerequisite to becoming a good investor is committing the time to do so. In other words, invest in yourself. You *can* achieve great investment returns, meet your financial goals, and beat the professional investors you would otherwise entrust your capital to. For many of us it's not a choice, but a necessity.

The
Warren Buffetts
Next Door

CHAPTER 1

Vagabond Value

Investor: Christopher Rees

Date of Birth: November 20, 1950

Hometown: Puerto Plata, Dominican Republic

Personal Web Site: www.tenstocks.com

Employment: Full-time investor, runs a subscription advisory

Passions/Pursuits: Workaholic, spends free time with wife and daughter

Investment Strategy: Deep value, special situations

Brokerage Accounts: TD Ameritrade

Key Strategy Metric: Tangible asset value

Online Haunts: www.marketocracy.com, www.valueinvestorsclub.com, www.10kwizard.com

Best Pick: Elan Corp., Up 143 percent

Worst Pick: Flag Telecom, Down 100 percent

Performance Since October 2000: Average annual return 25 percent versus 0.21 percent for the S&P 500[1]

S ubsistence living is something that most of us never even consider. Living on the edge of poverty is, after all, the stuff of nightmares. It's the downside we try never to think about.

But for nearly 30 years of his life Christopher Rees thought about subsistence living or "just getting by" nearly every day. Understanding his downside was a way of life. From age 19 to 49, Christopher Rees was a vagabond, moving around the globe from city to city, working in low-paying jobs, earning just enough to keep him going until his next stop. He became masterful at understanding how to stretch a dollar.

In fact, figuring out the bare minimums of survival became a religion for Rees. It is a lifestyle that also set the foundation for Chris Rees's highly successful investment style.

Since October 2000 Chris Rees's Marketocracy.com portfolio (10STX) has logged an average annual return of 25 percent compared to less than 1 percent for the S&P 500 (see Figure 1.1). This impressive record incorporates a 40 percent loss during the financial meltdown of

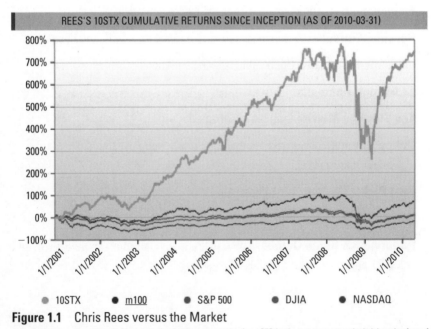

Figure 1.1   Chris Rees versus the Market

Note: Returns are after all implied fees including 5c/share transaction fees; SEC feeds; management and administration fees of 19.5 percent.

Source: Marketocracy.com; data as of March 31, 2010.

2008. It would be difficult to find a skilled hedge fund pro with Rees's stats. Among his closed stock positions, 89 percent have been winners.

Central to Rees's investment strategy is figuring out what a company's true net worth is. That means stripping out all of the fluff that is prevalent on CPA-certified corporate balance sheets.

Tangible asset value, real earnings, and debt levels are what Rees obsesses about. Just as he did during his vagabond days, he wants to know the bare minimums for a company's survival so he can determine the risk he faces investing in a stock. Chris Rees wants to know the downside—the worst case. And if a stock is selling at 50 percent of what he reckons its value is, then he buys. Rees's motto is taken right from the pages of Warren Buffett's playbook. Simply, "Don't lose money."

Tangible Tactics

In a connected, always-on world where time is a precious resource and complexity and multitasking have become a way of life, Chris Rees is an unapologetic heretic.

He simply will not abide by this lifestyle, and this attitude infuses into his investment strategy. Life has a slower, simpler pace in the Dominican Republic where Rees resides. Temperatures rarely get below 70 degrees Fahrenheit, and the heat and humidity make siestas a way of life. It is a culture where patience is a prerequisite and "mañana" may be the most common refrain.

Simplicity is also a virtue for Rees, and when it comes to investing, Rees's objective is to have only 10 stocks in his portfolio at any one time. This is not unlike other famous "deep value" investors like Warren Buffett and hedge fund managers Seth Klarman of Baupost Group and David Einhorn of Greenlight Capital.

These legendary value managers run concentrated portfolios. The idea is to own stocks as though they are businesses and to have a deep knowledge of all aspects of the companies' operations, potential prospects, and pitfalls.

Strategy Tip

Though financial advisors lecture clients on the importance of diversification, many of the most successful investors like Chris Rees manage concentrated portfolios with relatively few holdings. Warren Buffett once said, "Diversification is protection against ignorance. It makes little sense for those who know what they are doing."

Says Rees, "I'm a one-man show. There's only one brain in this office. I know investment managers, and I see them on the TV, they run a 200-stock portfolio. To me it's simply nuts. I work a lot of hours because I love my work. But I don't think you can follow more than 10 stocks well."

Chris Rees says that he gets his ideas from a slew of sources and is reluctant to give specifics, but he clearly uses stock screening software and alert services from web sites like the old 10kwizard.com (now called Morningstar Document Research) and SecInfo.com to cull through official SEC filings for certain fundamental characteristics.

"I may be looking for one or two investments a year," says Rees. "I've got a universe of 10,000-plus companies, so I'm throwing companies over my shoulder like a maniac. Anything that doesn't sniff right is eliminated, until I finish up with one company."

At the heart of Rees's strategy is his extreme aversion to losing money, or protecting his downside. Says Rees, "My basic philosophy is that I don't believe successful investing is about finding stuff that goes up. I think it's about finding stuff that's not going to go down."

To this end Rees is obsessive about determining a company's tangible asset value, also known as its tangible book value. In conversation he sometimes refers to it as liquidation value.

Tangible asset value is defined as a company's assets minus its liabilities. However, deducted from those assets are the fuzzy things that tend to inflate the number such as "goodwill," which might measure the value of brands acquired during an acquisition. Another intangible asset that Rees might deduct is his estimation for obsolete inventory. In general, Rees is looking for companies that are selling at a price that is significantly lower than his estimation of its tangible asset value per share.

Strategy Tip

Rees cautions investors not to confuse his tangible asset value with the book value figures that are commonly quoted on dozens of web sites, including Yahoo Finance. Book value can be inflated by intangibles like goodwill or obsolete inventory. "Book value is too dodgy, squishy," says Rees.

The next thing Rees looks at when investigating a potential stock to buy is its balance sheet, or debt levels. "I don't like debt. I don't want anything to do with debt," he says. "Any business, any CEO who loads up on debt, I'm not interested." Rees mostly focuses on a company's debt-to-equity ratio, which he says shouldn't exceed 50 percent.

The last thing Rees looks at in his relatively simple strategy is earnings. "The company has got to be profitable or I have to see a pathway to profitability." Rees often looks for turnarounds and other special situations. Thus if Rees likes the long-term prospects of a company that will lose money for the next several quarters, before turning profitable, Rees will discount its tangible asset value by a multiple of its losses.

Here's a basic explanation of how Rees determines value. Say Rees finds a company with low debt and figures out that its tangible asset value is $5 per share. If his estimate for forward earnings per share was $0.10 he might apply a price-earnings multiple of 10 to that. That would amount to $1 of future earnings value, so Chris would simply add the two to get a $6 estimated fair value for the stock. He would then seek to purchase it at a 50 percent discount to that value, or $3. If the stock price was too high, he would simply move on to the next candidate.

As part of Rees's "go anywhere" deep value strategy, he often seeks special situations where he believes the stock's true potential is misunderstood. One such special situation he's made a killing on is Elan Corp. (NYSE: ELN). Rees first became interested in the biotech company in 2005 after its multiple sclerosis drug Tysabri was abruptly pulled from the market. Apparently, one of the patients taking Tysabri died of a rare brain infection. Elan's stock plummeted to $3 from $30.

Rees did some digging to find out that the medical records revealed that part of the problem revolved around the patient taking the drug in conjunction with other medications and that the problem patient had a compromised immune system.

"Shares were trading on emotion and misinformation. I was a buyer into the fear and panic, which wasn't easy at the time," says Rees. "I thought Tysabri would come back, perhaps with a stiffer label, but the risk/reward benefit to the patient was significant." Rees bought Elan's distressed shares starting in 2005 as it was recovering. Elan's been a volatile stock ever since, and Rees has skillfully traded in and out of it.

According to Marketocracy, Elan has accounted for $2.7 million of the gains on Rees's million dollar virtual portfolio, which had a total value of $8.3 million as of the beginning of 2010.

Of course not all of Rees's picks have been homeruns like Elan. In late 2000 Rees bought into the distressed shares of Flag Telecom,[2] an Indian company that was laying fiber-optic cable under the sea for countries in the Middle East, Europe, and Asia. "I thought this was a valuable asset and it would stay out of bankruptcy. Even if it filed I thought there were enough tangible assets and cash for the common stock to be worth something."

However, in 2001 Flag filed for Chapter 11 bankruptcy, and common stockholders were wiped out. Rees learned a valuable lesson about distressed asset investing.

"I saw first hand how bankruptcy law is used and abused using the wonder of 'fresh start' accounting. So, my interest now is more in who is in bankruptcy currently and who is likely to emerge with 'fresh start' value. Bankruptcy investing is fascinating." Indeed, Rees cites Wilbur Ross, the well-known billionaire bankruptcy investor, among his investing role models.

In late 2009, Rees bought the post-bankruptcy shares of commercial finance and leasing company CIT Group (NYSE: CIT) for about $25. As of April 2010 its stock had risen to $40.

Who Is Chris Rees?

Chris Rees was born in 1950 in Stony Stratford, England, a small picturesque town about 90 minutes northeast of London. Stony Stratford dates back to Roman times, but it's best known for being the birthplace of the proverbial "cock and bull story." In the eighteenth century, two of Stony's pubs, the Cock and the Bull, were known to host travelers going between London and Liverpool who would gossip and tell outlandish tales. To this day Stony still hosts storytelling and humor festivals celebrating Cock and Bull's legacy.

The "Saga of Chris Rees" certainly deserves a place in Stony's colorful history. Rees's start in life was tortured because as a young child he suffered from severe allergies and eczema. As he recalls it, he spent from ages 5 to 10 confined to a hospital. "I was basically getting eaten alive with eczema," he says. "The strategy in those days was to take a five-year-old kid and spread-eagle him out on a bed, tying him to the four corners and basically leave him there," quips

Rees. "I made a decision that if I ever got out of that place, I was never going back. So I thought the best way of making sure of this was to get the hell out of Dodge, be an independent person."

So upon being released from the hospital at age 10, Rees began dreaming of his departure from Stony Stratford. His teachers didn't think much of him, and as he puts it he was pegged for a career in "shoveling horse manure onto loganberry plants." The only subject he seemed to excel at was geography.

In the middle to late 1960s, when Rees was finishing up high school, British authorities decided that they would create a new planned city called Milton Keynes just a few miles from Stony that would house hundreds of thousands of city dwellers being over-crowded in London. Rees saw this as an opportunity to earn money for the "escape" he was planning. So Rees took up selling household appliances to builders and contractors developing the vast suburban housing tracts of Milton Keynes. He also worked in odd jobs like furniture and carpet sales, saving for his departure.

Rees finally accumulated enough money for his travels by wagering his boss on a Chelsea versus Leeds United FA Cup final soccer match in 1970. Rees told his boss that he would leave if his team, Chelsea, won. After tying initially, Chelsea beat Leeds in a heated replay match 2 to 1. Rees collected his winnings and left for Spain.

"My mum thought I would make it about 10 miles down the road and get homesick and come back," say Rees. However, this was the beginning of a nearly three-decades-long journey in which Rees wandered through some 30 countries around the globe. Hippie culture was in full bloom, and being a flower child and living a nomadic lifestyle had great appeal to Rees. "The idea was to live as frugally and cheaply as I could and to make the trip last as long as I could. I had to spend close to zero money and pick up odd jobs that would keep me going," says Rees.

So Rees washed dishes, waited tables, and worked on construction sites while traveling throughout Europe. Every few years he would return to England to work factory jobs for a few months and save money for his next adventure. However, eventually Rees figured out that Switzerland was a better place to sojourn and earn money. "I knew the Swiss franc was very strong and I could do carpentry there, sleep on a friend's couch, save money and then go to places like India, or Yugoslavia, or Central America, and it was like having three times the amount of cash in your pocket."

In Switzerland, Rees installed saunas in homes. In Amritsar, Punjab, India, Rees was a cook in a restaurant, sleeping on a mat on the kitchen floor at night. In Kandahar, Afghanistan, Rees worked as a tailor wearing a traditional turban and *salwar kameez* helping to make three-piece men's polyester business suits, mostly for export to Iran. In Belize, he was an eco-tour operator and charter boat captain.

Finally Rees made his way to the United States, traveling around in a secondhand Volkswagen bus. By the time Rees made it to California, his VW engine was shot. Without any money for repairs, Rees ended up sleeping in his bus in a trailer park on a Native American Reservation just across the Colorado River in Yuma, Arizona, wondering what to do next.

One night Rees ended up at a saloon down the road where they were playing poker in a backroom. Rees was intrigued and eventually he learned to play Lowball Poker, a game in which the worst hand wins. Chris Rees had a good understanding of odds—back in England his father had been a bookmaker and Rees remembered watching him at the chalkboard change odds based on the "book" or betting interest in the horses as the race time drew near. Chris Rees became so good at this variation of poker that the tavern owner employed him to play for the house.

One evening, while playing with the money that he had earned, one of the players at his table threw the keys to his 1965 Cadillac Sedan DeVille into the pot as the stakes got higher. Rees had the worst and winning hand—five cards with six high. Rees had what he needed to continue on his journeys, so he packed up his new Caddy and started to make his way to Florida.

By the time he arrived in Tampa, Rees had run out of money again. So he slept in his car on the beach at night and was about to give up and figure out a way back to England when he was offered a job in the kitchen of a restaurant. He took it and rose from dishwasher to cook to kitchen manager and was making enough money to share a rented apartment.

By the middle of the 1980s, Rees's yearning for adventure led him to buy a 33-foot sailboat with the idea that he would teach himself to sail and explore the Caribbean by boat. Rees figured it was the best way to travel that part of the world, given that you didn't have to pay for airline travel or hotels. After work each day, Rees headed to the local library and read dozens of sailing books until he felt ready to set sail.

Rees spent the next 14 years traveling in the Florida Keys, Central America, and the Caribbean Islands in his sloop, the *Trilogy*, supporting himself mostly by giving "eco-tours" and sailing excursions. "In sailing you learn to stay safe. Screwing up or putting yourself in a bad place at a bad time can cost you your life," says Rees reflecting on his years at sea. "Risk analysis becomes second nature."

While Chris Rees was sailing around the Florida Keys he developed a toothache that would change his life.

Sitting in the dental office in excruciating pain, Rees became fed up with waiting and went looking for the dentist whom he found hunched over a computer screen in his office tending to his stock portfolio. Rees was fascinated by what he was doing and made it his point to learn more about investing.

Rees became a regular at the Marathon public library in the Florida Keys, reading everything he could on investing and eventually learning how to navigate web sites like Yahoo Finance with the library's computer. He managed to invest small sums of his savings through a Schwab brokerage account and became addicted to publications like *Barron's*.

During one of his stints giving eco-tours on the Rio Dulce in Guatemala, Rees paid a series of local merchants and couriers to bring him a *Barron's* each week from a hotel in Guatemala City to his sailboat far down the river via dug-out canoe. "It was like waiting for God to arrive," recalls Rees.

Ultimately, as Rees was approaching 50, he began to tire of his adventures. "I had been doing this my whole life; save $5,000, go traveling for a year then become penniless and start all over again," he says. "It's wonderful when you're young, but you've got to get a bit practical."

So Rees decided that if he could save up $50,000 in capital, he could probably live modestly in one of his favorite destinations, the Dominican Republic. His plan was to manage an investment portfolio and produce an average annual return of 15 percent. "I knew if I started and I had a bad first year, it might never work, but I thought if I'm really, really careful and really disciplined and treat it like a business, then I could get my 15 percent."

Rees worked two jobs to save $30,000 over the course of a few years, all the while learning about investing and using the Internet at the library in Marathon. In October 2000 Rees joined the Web stock picking community Marketocracy.com and created a million-dollar virtual portfolio to test his skills and see how he measured up against others. A few months later, Rees sold his 33-foot sloop for $20,000 and bought a ticket for the Dominican Republic, $50,000 cash in hand.

"The Dominican Republic fits me like an old tee shirt. It's a nutty place. It's almost the country that Monty Python would have invented," says Rees. With his $50,000 nest egg ready for investing, Rees rented a three-bedroom house with a two-car garage, electricity and cable TV, in the countryside outside of Puerto Plata for $84 per month. His 26kbps Internet access cost an additional $30 per month.

Nearly a decade later, Rees lives comfortably as a full-time investor. His real-life personal portfolio is similar to his virtual one on Marketocracy except for the fact that he occasionally uses leverage. Rees and his Dominican wife Isabel and six-year-old daughter Tina live in a spacious apartment on the North coast of the Dominican Republic, about 200 yards from the beach with views of the Caribbean Sea. The Rees family has four computers, and a satellite dish keeps Rees connected to the Internet at a speed of 1.5 megabytes per second. Rees runs a small subscription alert service and owns investment properties in the Puerta Plata area that he intends to develop.

Rees admits he is singularly devoted to his investing portfolio except for the time he spends with his wife and daughter going to the beach or eating out. Rees drives his daughter to school every day in a 1988 Jeep Cherokee, which he bought second hand. With age, and maturity, Rees's wanderlust seems to have fizzled. He is staying put. He no longer owns a boat or yearns for exotic foreign adventure.

Rees's Rules of Investing

Buy Rules

- Find companies with low debt, less than 50 percent of equity.
- Focus on tangible asset value (also known as tangible book value) and be mindful of intangibles that can inflate asset values.
- Look at realistic forward earnings potential.

Sell Rules

- Take profits if the stockholding approaches your estimated fair value.
- Sell if market-, sector-, or company-specific risk increases.
- Sell if the stock becomes overweighted in the portfolio.
- Sell if you find a better, lower-risk investment.
- Take profits if you can lower your overall portfolio risk by reallocating capital.

Case Study: Abatix Corp (OTC: ABIX)

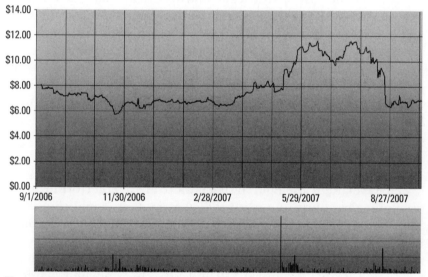

Figure 1.2   Abatix Corp, September 2006–September 2007
Source: © TickerTech.com, 2010.

Though Elan has been Chris Rees's best single pick to date, he claims that his success is mostly based on "hitting singles," buying low-risk/high-probability value stocks where he might book 30 percent plus gains. A good portion of Rees's investments are in the micro-cap arena, either because the companies are small or because they are distressed.

Abatix is an example of this (see Figure 1.2). Back in 2006 Rees had an investment in an oil exploration company operating in the Gulf of Mexico, but he wanted to somehow hedge against hurricanes, which are a real risk to these companies. So Rees discovered Abatix either through screens or an article he read online.

The firm, based in Mesquite, Texas, is a supplier of environmental products, and safety equipment firms prosper during disasters. Hurricanes, wildfires, pandemics, and terror attacks are good for its business because it sells things like fire retardant jumpsuits, high-visibility safety vests, dehumidifiers, and water and air filtration systems.

Rees downloaded Abatix's SEC filings and after doing some calculating, he figured that its tangible asset value per share was $6.75, mostly in the form of inventory and receivables.

In 2005, the year of Hurricane Katrina, Abatix had banner earnings of $1.22 a share. Rees calculated that normalized earnings for Abatix would be around $0.35 a share. He estimated this amount by using its last five years of reported earnings as a benchmark.

Says Rees, "I generally assign an estimated fair value on a company based on the value of net tangible assets plus a ten multiple on estimated forward run rate earnings." Thus Abatix was worth $10.25 on a no-disaster, no-chaos basis, according to Rees:

$$\$6.75 + \$3.50 = \$10.25$$

However, Rees also figured that if there was a bioterrorism attack or another big hurricane or earthquake, earnings could climb to a $1 or more per share, which when added to his tangible book value would give Abatix an upper end share price of $16. (*Indeed in late 2005 Abatix shares reached a high of $18.50.*) So Rees settled on a fair value for Abatix between $10 and $16. He purchased shares in November 2006 for an average cost of $6.25 and sold the stock seven months later for $11.10, a 78 percent gain.

Rees
In His Own Words

Reflecting on the Financial Meltdown of 2008

I have just finished the worst year in my history.

My model fund at Marketocracy ended the year down 42 percent. It is remarkable that I was still positive (up 8 percent) as late as September 22nd. But to lose over half a portfolio in two months really takes some doing, but I managed it.

While getting my head handed to me in 2008, I was not alone. I had some very good company. Warren Buffett's Berkshire Hathaway (NYSE: BRK-A) (a holding in my model fund until late 2007) fell around 45 percent from its 2007 high. Martin Whitman's Third Avenue Value Fund (TAVFX) was down 46 percent for the year. Bill Miller, of Legg Mason Value Trust (LMVTX), and famous for out-performing the S&P 500 for 15 years straight, finished the year down 55 percent. There were so many violent twists and turns in 2008 that very few people got it right and of those who did, a lot of them STILL lost a lot of money.

Buffett has said, "Predicting rain doesn't count; building arks does." I clearly didn't build an ark, and I can be faulted for that. But I did have anchors to windward. But when the Category 7 hurricane of October/November came, nothing held.

We have had a jarring and painful 2008. I have received many e-mails, especially in Q4, expressing understandable concern. Overall, you have been truly wonderful. I thank you for your support and continued trust in me.

Also, I am a strong believer in keeping my mouth shut and letting the results do the talking. Over the long term, the results have generally spoken favorably. I spend a lot of time reading opinions, articles, and reports. I listen to talking heads on Bloomberg. Ninety percent of everything I read, see, and hear is total garbage and an utter waste of time. Not too long ago I told someone that "increasingly investors will need to produce more return on their capital and with conventional mutual funds wallowing in mediocrity it becomes a smart proposition to at least consider alternative methods and vehicles where the emphasis is less on the talk and more on the walk." In 2007 and now in 2008, there hasn't been much *walk*. But I still don't like talking. When I have a reasonable year, I don't usually do a year-end letter. For 2008, it's all I've got.

—January 3, 2009, Marketocracy.com

CHAPTER 2

Options Apostle

Investor: Bob Krebs

Date of Birth: July 24, 1952

Hometown: Orange County, CA

Personal Web Site: None

Employment: Engineer, computer storage business

Passions/Pursuits: Bible study, jazz lover, coaching his daughters' speech and debating team, budding novelist

Investment Strategy: Income investing for total return using put and call options

Brokerage Accounts: Charles Schwab, Fidelity, E*Trade

Key Strategy Metric: Yield

Online Haunts: www.valueforum.com

Best Pick: Cisco, Up 800 percent

Worst Pick: Deep Sea Supply Plc., Down 80 percent

Performance Since September 2005: Cumulative return of 287 percent versus 11 percent for the S&P 500[1]

For many of us investing in stocks is fairly one-dimensional. Buy stocks of companies you think will appreciate and, ideally, sell them after they've gone up in price. Some people trade frequently, but most are buy-and-hold investors. Few are good at either of these strategies. Only a small number of investors ever venture into such exotic tactics as shorting stocks or trading options. Most are either too afraid of the risks involved or bewildered by the additional math skills required to execute these strategies well.

Proficiency in mathematics was never an issue for Bob Krebs, an electrical engineer and next-generation microchip designer for Western Digital. Still, investment success did not come overnight for Krebs. He describes himself as a 34-year student of investing and markets. His experience includes investing in California's real estate boom, surviving Black Monday and the dot-com bubble as well as the 2008 financial crisis.

However, today at age 58, Krebs has settled on an opportunistic strategy that seeks to produce steadily flowing income from his investments boosting the overall total return on what might otherwise be a run-of-the-mill stock portfolio. Krebs practices his craft mostly using high-yielding dividend stocks in conjunction with call and put options. On average he devotes about four hours of each day to his portfolio.

On a typical day Krebs wakes up early to log into ValueForum .com, a small subscription Web community that fosters idea sharing and investor education, before heading to work in Orange County, CA. Think of ValueForum as an intelligent and focused alternative to the Yahoo Finance message boards. Its members discuss investment ideas and themes, and teach each other about their investment successes and failures.

According to ValueForum, which has held quarterly stock-picking contests dating back to 2004, $10,000 invested in Krebs's quarterly stock picks would have appreciated to $38,700 as of March 31, 2010 (see Figure 2.1). That compares to $11,100 had you invested your money in an ETF or mutual fund that tracked the S&P 500.

Krebs's real-life portfolio returns have been even more impressive. On ValueForum he has been reporting his actual portfolio returns dating back to 2003, and, according to his postings, he has logged an impressive compounded average annual return of 25 percent. During 2009 Krebs managed to nearly match the S&P

500 return with a 25 percent total return, even though at least 50 percent of his portfolio was parked in cash during the entire year. But it's not just his sheer performance numbers and portfolio returns that make Krebs an outstanding investor.

Among ValueForum's 1,200 members, Bob Krebs, or "dig4Value" as he is known online, is highly regarded as a teacher. On the site's ratings system he gets its highest, gold star rating, meaning other community members value his advice above the vast majority of others. In fact, each year when ValueForum holds its annual "Invest-fest" member conference in places like Orlando or Las Vegas, Krebs preaches the gospel of enhancing portfolio returns using options in an hour-long workshop.

ValueForum members who attend Krebs's crash course in options sit attentively soaking in every word and slide in his presentation. With his glasses, goatee, pocket pens and Wall Street-themed necktie, Krebs comes off as a nerdy stock guru.

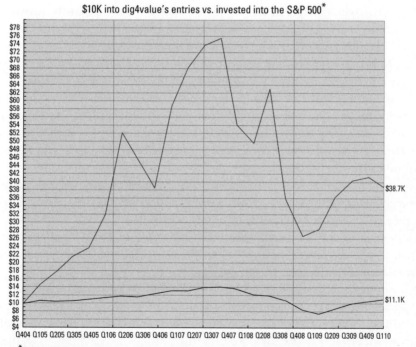

$10K into dig4value's entries vs. invested into the S&P 500*

*Calculated by investing into the first contest entry; cashing out the positions at the end of the contest; investing the proceeds into the next contest entry, and so on.

Figure 2.1   Bob Krebs versus the Market

Source: © TickerTech.com, 2010; data as of March 31, 2010, dig4value = Bob Kreb's screen name on ValueForum.com.

Sell Options, Have Fun, and Make Money

Mathematically minded Krebs is a man who likes to measure odds. "When I first started in options, most of the time I was on the buy-side, purchasing calls," says Krebs. "But I soon realized that was a losing game."

Krebs did some research and found out that most call option buyers actually lost money. In fact, he discovered that 75 percent of all calls purchased expire unexercised or worthless. The stats look even worse for those who buy put options—83 percent of put options expire worthless.[2]

Krebs had an investing epiphany. "I said to myself, if options are a zero-sum game, then options sellers are the ones making the money and I need to become a seller of puts and calls."

A *call option* is an agreement or contract that gives an investor the right to purchase a specified amount of stock at a specified price (strike price) within a specific time period (expiration date). A *put option* gives an investor the right to sell a specified amount of a stock at a specified price within a specified time period.[3] Option sellers or "writers" are paid a premium from buyers for the right (but not obligation) to buy or sell the underlying stock.

To be sure, Krebs has never given up buying and holding straight equities, especially high yield dividend stocks and trusts. However, he now enhances this strategy by selling options with three goals in mind—to generate income, to buy into stocks he likes at bargain prices, and to manage his equity risk. Or as he flippantly advises other ValueForum members, "Sell some options, have fun, and make some money."

At first, Krebs focused almost exclusively on a strategy known as *covered call writing.* Covered call writing is one of the least risky of all options strategies because it allows investors the chance to generate income from stocks they would otherwise have sitting in their portfolios. In options jargon being "covered" means that you have possession of the underlying securities needed if the option is ever exercised. As Krebs puts it, covered call writing is profitable 80 percent of the time.

Say, for example, Krebs has a long-term holding of 1,000 shares of IBM (NYSE: IBM) that he purchased at $100 per share. Total invested, $100,000. Krebs's goal for his long-term portfolio holdings of IBM might be to use options to generate at least 8 percent in additional income above and beyond the dividends his stock might pay.

So Krebs would typically seek out call options that are far "out-of-the-money," meaning that they are at strike prices higher than IBM's current price and are thus unlikely to be exercised. If IBM's stock tends to trade in a range of say $90 and $110, then Krebs would look to sell 10 call option contracts, each representing the right to buy 100 shares, at a strike price of $115 and an expiration three months out. That would give the buyer of these options the right to buy Krebs's 1,000 shares of IBM from him at a price of $115. If the quoted options price were $3, each contract would be worth $300 and 10 would be worth $3,000. Since Krebs is *selling* these calls he would receive $3,000 deposited in his brokerage account.

If Krebs is correct and IBM's price doesn't climb above $115, or more than 15 percent in the ensuing three months, those call options he sold would expire worthless, and Krebs would profit by the $3,000 premium he received. He would then try to repeat this every three months, adjusting his pricing accordingly. If he can do this successfully, he can generate $12,000 or 12 percent in extra income on that $100,000 in IBM stock that is otherwise sitting in his portfolio.

If Krebs is wrong and IBM soars, the investor he sold his options to will exercise his right to buy Krebs's 1,000 shares of IBM, and Krebs will be closed out of his position at a price of $115,000. Krebs would get to keep the $3,000 he initially received for selling the calls. His gain would be $18,000 or 18 percent.

The only losing scenario in covered call writing is if IBM's shares fall below Krebs's $100 purchase price, but then again Krebs's losses are cushioned by the $3,000 or $3 per share premium he got. Thus Krebs doesn't start to lose money until IBM falls below $97 per share.

Another option strategy that Krebs likes to employ he calls *naked short puts.* "It sounds very exotic and risky, but from a risk/

Strategy Tip

Options are quoted as *contracts*. Each contract controls 100 shares of underlying stock, thus investors get the magnifying affect of leverage when trading options. You can find detailed information on call and put options premium pricing, sometimes called option chains, on most e-broker web sites as well as www.finance.yahoo.com and www.schaeffersresearch.com.

reward basis it is the theoretical equivalent of a covered call strategy," says Krebs. The term *naked* is used in options trading to refer to a situation where the options writer or seller does not have a position in the underlying stock or instrument.

Say Krebs is bullish on gold and he wants to buy shares of Yamana Gold (NYSE: AUY), currently trading at $13. Krebs ideally would like to get the shares cheaper, say at $11.50. He could call his broker and put in a good-till canceled limit order for the stock at $11.50, hoping that it will fall in price to that level. Or he could sell put options for Yamana with a strike price of $12, which might be trading at $0.50 a share.

Thus if Yamana's stock price drops below $12 Krebs will be forced to purchase the underlying stock from the person he sold his "naked" puts to but his cost will be $12 minus the $0.50 per share he received as a premium. Therefore he would own the stock at his goal price of $11.50.

Now if Yamana didn't fall below $12 or went up, Krebs keeps the $0.50 per share premium in income he got for selling the options in the first place.

Using these two core options strategies, Krebs seeks to earn from 1.5 percent to 3 percent *in extra income* from his stock portfolio each month, augmenting the total return he gets. Indeed, Krebs admits that he typically has positions in 50 to 200 options contracts at any given time.

Who Is Bob Krebs?

Krebs was raised in Tucson, Arizona, the son of an electrician. At age 14 Krebs's family moved to Southern California, and ultimately he graduated from University of California, Irvine, with a degree in electrical engineering. "My dad was a blue collar guy," says Krebs. "My family always rented, so the first thing I did when I got out

Strategy Tip

Krebs recommends starting slow with options, first on "paper" and then by using covered strategies. Your broker will require you to answer questionnaires gauging your investment knowledge and experience before allowing you to trade options in your account.

of college was stayed home for two years, and saved and bought a place."

Krebs had landed an entry-level position with IBM competitor Burroughs Corporation in Pasadena and purchased a condominium in the Claremont/Pomona area. "My goal was to leverage this and buy an investment property every three years."

Krebs did just that. He bought single-family homes in Orange County enclaves like Mission Viejo and San Juan Capistrano using a technique known as "80-10-10." Krebs would put down 10 percent of the purchase price, and the owner would offer him a five-year note for 10 percent of the price thus avoiding the need for expensive private mortgage insurance required by lenders when a buyer puts down less than 20 percent. With California housing prices on the rise, it was easy for Krebs to either refinance his loans within five years or sell the property at a profit. Krebs rode California's real estate market through the late 1970s and 1980s buying and selling five properties.

All the while Krebs had a keen interest in stocks and options and began dabbling in them with his free capital. When *Investor's Business Daily* was founded in 1984, Krebs became a charter subscriber investing in stocks on the famed IBD 100. Krebs liked these momentum stocks, and as a tech industry insider he witnessed the birth of such innovative companies as Xilinx, Altera, Cisco Systems, and Dell Computer. These stocks, as well as others like Intel, became staples of Krebs's portfolio.

On Sunday afternoons Krebs would spend hours cutting out the charts of stocks on the IBD 100 and paste them onto pieces of paper so that he could keep notes on them. His research filled up a four-inch loose-leaf binder, which was supplemented by a large spreadsheet he kept on his personal computer.

Just as he had done in California housing, Krebs began to ride the technology boom using technical analysis to determine when to buy and sell the stocks he held. Each morning he would wake at 5:30 Pacific time and watch the premarket and market open. He would normally spend an hour making trades before he left for work at 7:30 a.m.

By the latter half of the 1990s Krebs found that he had amassed 60 percent of his equity portfolio—which was now several hundred thousand dollars—in a single stock, wireless hardware company Cisco Systems (NASDAQ: CSCO).

"I know that sounds crazy, but it was a very good strategy. They were the big gorilla in their space, and they had a good-sized moat," says Krebs referring to Warren Buffett's philosophy of buying companies relatively impervious to competition.

However, while doing some research on his largest holding in 1999, Krebs began to see a pattern in Cisco's results that made him nervous.

"About every quarter, Cisco would purchase a few little techno companies in its space, and simply say they were one-time events so they didn't have to hit their bottom line.[4] They would do this constantly and claim that they were extraordinary items," says Krebs, who adds, "Another trick they had was that John Chambers (Cisco's CEO) used to go on CNBC every quarter and announce that they beat earnings by a penny."

Krebs crunched the numbers and realized that if one were to include Cisco's "extraordinary items," which seemed to be recurring, its earnings would be flat to down.

"'A big lightbulb went off. I had 60 percent of my net worth in Cisco,' I said to myself, 'This thing is going to fall apart!'"

So Krebs contacted 15 investor friends he had been communicating with via e-mail, explained his analysis and told them, "I'm getting out."

That was December 1999 when Cisco shares had risen to as high as $50 per share. Krebs ultimately sold out of Cisco within 15 percent of its peak price of $79 per share in March 2000. "This is what saved me from getting completely annihilated in the dot-com crash," says Krebs who admits that he suffered big losses on most of the other stocks in his technology-heavy portfolio.

Krebs's tech stock losses were a double-whammy because the start-up he was then working for ran into trouble in the aftermath of the tech bubble. In May 2002 at the nadir of the post-9/11 stock market, Krebs found himself out of work.

So at age 50, Krebs decided to take the summer off before seeking another engineering job. It was about that time that Krebs happened upon a message board on Yahoo Finance for a stock, which had been delisted, but Yahoo had neglected to remove the online forum. A few smart value investors had been using the abandoned online forum known as the "TIE" board to share ideas and communicate.

The board's users, many of whom were retirees, had an approach to investing that was very different from the one that

Krebs was used to. For these investors dividends or yield was paramount.

"They were smarter than the pros in what they covered, and I got excited about this. I spent a whole summer learning from them. Then I began rebuilding my portfolio in this completely different manner," says Krebs, who proceeded to buy REITs, Canadian energy trusts, shipping stocks, and other commodity-based equities. Krebs also bought into subprime lenders like Novastar Financial and Impac Mortgage Holdings, which were throwing off huge dividend yields.

"At the time, these were stocks that nobody even discussed or cared about. You would never see them mentioned in the newspaper," says Krebs.

Eventually Krebs joined ValueForum.com, an online stock community created in 2003 for investors like him who were sharing ideas on certain inactive Yahoo stock message boards. Initially this small group of investors solicited two recent college graduates, Adam Menzel and Ben Nobel, to build a private Web-based community for them. The idea was to have an online stock community free from the touting and noise associated with most online chat rooms, like Yahoo, Raging Bull and The Motley Fool.

ValueForum would be open to all, but members would need to pay a fee, which now stands at $250 per year. Today 1,200 avid stock investors trade ideas, debate stocks, participate in contests, poll each other, and rate recommendations. Krebs doesn't hesitate to tell anyone who asks that the members of ValueForum are his primary source for ideas and research. Most members contribute ideas and news, and generally add to the knowledge base of the community. Many like Krebs are happy to educate novices in their particular areas of expertise. Krebs, aka dig4value, spends up to four hours per day on the web site and is called on for his options expertise.

With interest rates generally at low levels, Krebs has been devoting more time to income-generating options strategies. Krebs typically limits his options activity to about 100 stocks that he watches closely. Often they are the same yield stocks he owns in his long portfolio.

"If I am happy owning a stock that is yielding 10 percent, why not see if I can write puts underneath it (out of the money) and pick up another 10 percent in premium income," says Krebs. "I always focus on the worst-case scenario. In this case, it would mean owning more of the stock at a cheaper price. It's sort of like putting in a stink bid and being paid to wait while I do this."

Though Krebs is passionate about investing he is also a devoted parent. His spare time is spent mostly with his teenage daughters, whom he and his wife, also an electrical engineer, have been home-schooling. Explains Krebs, "While we could afford to send our kids to private schools, we really look at them as our most precious asset and therefore don't want to give other individuals the opportunity to spend the bulk of our children's time during the day with them, as opposed to us."

Like many other homeschoolers, the Krebs's are devout Christians. Krebs's wife is responsible for most of his high school–aged girls' primary tutoring, but Krebs spends his weekends coaching his daughters and other teens at their church in debating and speech giving. In fact, Krebs's daughters are leading competitors in the National Christian Forensics Communications Association (NCFCA) speech and debate tournaments. These events promote analytical and oratorical skills, addressing issues with a "Biblical world view." Krebs recently completed his first novel (a thriller) in which the protagonist is a homeschooled teenager.

The Krebs's do not tolerate network or cable television in their home but do use their television to watch an occasional movie. "When people ask me how I do so well in the stock market, I say that the first thing you have to do is get rid of your television set," says Krebs. However, showing a bit of his "geek" roots, he adds, "I will admit that we do have more computers in our house than salient beings, including enough for our fish and dog."

Krebs's Rules of Investing

- **Make sure you aren't trying to impose your ego on the market.**
  According to Krebs this important rule has a corollary that says avoid at all costs taking a large loss on any single security. When fundamental investors buy stocks, they do so, according to Krebs, with two currencies. One is in the form of the hard dollars they spend to buy their shares and the other is in the form of emotional currency. After all, most serious individual investors spend a good deal of time researching a stock, believing in its story and expecting that they will be rewarded when they are proven correct. "You are

putting your emotional opinion on the line as much as you are spending the money," says Krebs.

But what if the market just doesn't agree with you, regardless of all the effort you have put into your research and the stock continues to go down? Krebs says investors need to swallow their pride and sell. He also warns of an even greater sin. *Never* double down and add to your holdings using the argument "The sellers are fools! I've done my research on this. The stock is even cheaper now!"

Krebs says that some professional value investors use this "nerves of steel" approach to buy stocks as they sink but says it is best left to the pros. "In a general sense, I would much, much rather be purchasing stocks as they go up," says Krebs.

Krebs learned this rule of investing the hard way. In the 1990s Krebs became emotionally tied up in his bullish position in MCI. "I felt that MCI was a solid company, and it was paying out a really fine dividend," says Krebs. The company and its chief Bernie Ebbers ultimately became mired in a fraud case. MCI went bankrupt, and Krebs lost about $50,000 in the stock and on the put options he was writing underneath his position.

Likewise in 2008 he let his ego get in the way of prudent investing in a stock called Deep Sea Supply (otc: DSSPF). It lost 80 percent of its value in six months. Deep Sea Supply is an offshore tug and supply vessel fleet owner controlled by Norwegian billionaire shipping magnate John Fredriksen. Krebs and a number of ValueForum members became enamored with the stock because of its strong growth and relatively high dividend yields. Deep Sea's dividend yield was running as high as 10 percent.

The economic slowdown and liquidity crisis in 2008 hit most shipping companies hard. Deep Sea's stock plummeted as trade-related business dried up and credit markets froze. In May 2008, Deep Sea cut its dividend to $0.13 from $0.40. While Deep Sea's stock was falling, Krebs argued to himself to hold on because the commissions for trading this foreign stock (Deep Sea is based in Cyprus) were as high as 5 percent.

"I used the cost of selling as an excuse to support my ego. That was crazy," says Krebs. He ultimately dumped the stock for a big loss though it was no "Cisco" and only represented about 9 percent of Krebs's portfolio in the beginning of 2008.

- **Sell when the 20-day moving average crosses below the 50-day moving average.**

Though Krebs is more value-oriented in his approach than he was during the years he read *Investor's Business Daily* religiously, he still likes to use technicals when investing. Krebs focuses on something called moving average convergence divergence, otherwise known as MACD. MACD lines show the difference between a fast and a slow exponential moving average (EMA) of closing prices. It's a momentum indicator that tracks the trend in a stock price. It is widely followed by investors, so Krebs pays attention to it. If a shorter-term MACD like the 20-day moving average crosses below a longer-term MACD, like the 50-day MACD, on substantial volume, it is a bearish sign.

Krebs demonstrates his use of MACD in experience with DryShips (NASDAQ: DRYS), a shipping stock popular among members of ValueForum and a stock that Krebs has traded in and out of. DryShips was a high flyer from 2006 to 2008, with a 600 percent-plus run up in price. However, Krebs noticed in the middle of 2008 that its 20-day exponential moving average (see Figure 2.2) had crossed below its 50-day EMA. DryShips was hovering around $82 per share. That was a clear sell signal for Krebs, and he liquidated his position. DryShips shares fell to as low as $3.50 by November 2008.

Krebs says that once he sees a stock's 20-day cross over its 50-day it's time to think about unloading it even if the stock is a good dividend payer. That brings up another important Krebs rule.

Strategy Tip

While Krebs swears by the investing ideas and education he derives from fellow members of ValueForum.com, he uses *StockCharts.com* for access to free stock charts chock-full of technicals from MACD to Bollinger bands. For novices StockCharts.com has a Chartschool for learning about technical analysis.

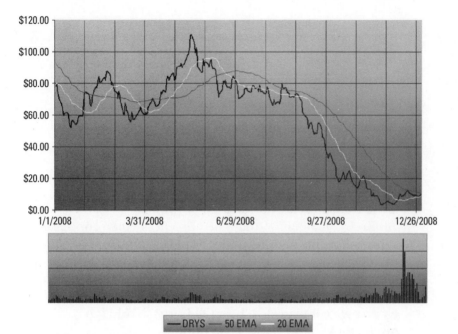

Figure 2.2   DryShips Inc (NASDAQ: DRYS), January 2008–December 2008
Source: © TickerTech.com, 2010.

- **Don't be lulled by a stock's dividend payment.**

  Krebs admits to making this mistake with Deep Sea Supply in 2008. Says Krebs, "I think it helps to own dividend stocks, and you can buffer yourself a little bit from losses with dividends. But I've seen many, many a dividend stock drop significantly beyond any recovery while still maintaining its dividend." Krebs argues that eventually the dividend may get cut, and by the time you find out it's too late.

  Krebs does assert that, all things being equal, it's prudent to find stocks that have a long history of maintaining and increasing dividends.

- **Don't be afraid to concentrate your portfolio.**

  Here Krebs is referring to something many professional value investors practice. (Chris Rees in Chapter 1 also abides by this rule.) The best way to create mediocre or index-like returns is to overdiversify. Says Krebs, "I would rather concentrate half of my portfolio and leave the rest in cash than try to diversify the whole amount because I believe the gains

Strategy Tip

Krebs prefers selling naked puts (naked short puts) to covered call writing on stocks in his portfolio. "Most people don't realize that from a risk/reward standpoint selling a naked put is the same as buying the stock and covering it by selling a call against it (covered calls). The difference is that you don't have to supply the money to buy the stock unless your put is exercised."

of concentrated portfolios can be substantially higher than those from a broadly diversified portfolio."

Krebs maintains that he practices the concentrated approach in his options trades as well. He often maintains 70 or 100 open contracts on options, but they are typically limited to a small number of underlying stocks. Thus Krebs might have open seven options contracts with different expirations on a single company like InterOil Corp. (NYSE: IOC).

• **Always look to buy back cheap options.**

Krebs warns that investors need to be very disciplined in options trading because they are more volatile than stocks. Thus investors need to weigh the risk associated with staying in an open options position all the way to expiration date. Says Krebs, "It's all a question of percentage gain versus time left. If you have 75 percent or 80 percent of the gain already, it's smart to buy an option back." Thus if Krebs sells a put for a $1.00 and over time it falls to being worth $0.20, Krebs will buy back the option even if there is a month or more left to expiration. This allows him to keep 80 percent of the premium he was expecting at expiration. Krebs advises investors to scour their options portfolio daily for opportunities to buy back cheap options. He describes this as a simple risk management technique.

"I don't wait until they expire because I can probably find a better investment for the remaining period of time with the margin requirement that I will have freed up. By closing out open options contracts, I am taking risk off the table," says Krebs.

As an example Krebs cites a recent position he had selling the puts options of a company called InterOil Corp. Krebs had written some puts on the stock and received a $2.50 premium. InterOil was rallying as the stock climbed to $50 per share. These specific puts fell in value to $0.45 each.

Krebs still had three months left until expiration on the options, but he bought back 50 of the contracts he owned and spent $2,250 doing so (50 contracts represent the right to 500 shares of the underlying stock and each contract cost Krebs $45, thus $45 × 50 = $2,250).

By closing his open short option position and locking in $2.05 in premium profit or $10,250 total on 50 contracts, Krebs simultaneously freed up $125,000 worth of equity margin requirement. That's because the 50 put contracts he had sold placed him on the hook for 5,000 shares in the underlying stock of IOC. That would have cost him $250,000 if he were forced by the put option he sold to buy the stock (highly unlikely given its rising price). Brokerage firms typically require 50 percent margin on stock purchases, so that 50 contract position forced Krebs to maintain $125,000 in equity in his account.

"The idea is that I should be able to find something else that would give me a better return than waiting for expiration. So I went out and sold more puts on that stock with a March expiration at a higher premium price, $4.80," says Krebs.

Case Study: Annaly Mortgage (NYSE: NLY)

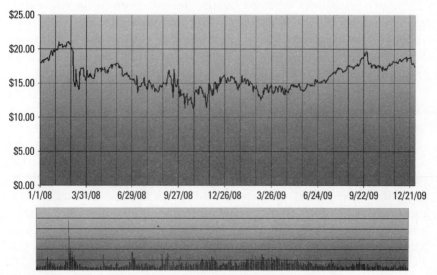

Figure 2.3 Annaly Mortgage, January 2008–December 2009

Source: © TickerTech.com, 2010.

Annaly Capital is a real estate investment trust specializing in mortgages. In the industry they are commonly called M-REITs, and their sole purpose is to generate income for their shareholders by investing in mortgage-backed securities. By law, REITs receive tax breaks, but they are compelled to distribute at least 90 percent of their income to shareholders in the form of dividends. Many investors love REITs for exactly this reason. There is little chance that self-dealing insiders or inept managers will squander company profits if 90 percent go to shareholders. As it happens, Annaly invests almost exclusively in mortgage-backed securities guaranteed by Fannie Mae, Freddie Mac, and Ginnie Mae.

During the financial crisis in 2008, Annaly's NYSE-listed shares (see Figure 2.3) got hit hard because it's in the mortgage business. Toxic subprime mortgages were making headlines daily so naturally anything related to mortgages was shunned. No one was sure if Fannie and Freddie were going to be allowed to fail the way Lehmann Brothers was, so Annaly's stock plummeted to around $12 per share from a high of $20.

But panic selling is music to a value investor's ears. Krebs first got interested in Annaly soon after its meltdown when two fellow members of the ValueForum stock community started posting comments about how they were accumulating shares. In mid-2008, two members that go by the screen names "Bonddaddy" and "Xstock," started recommending its shares. Both of these two ValueForum members had professional careers in the investment business, and, according to Krebs, their insights were always spot on.

Bonddaddy and Xstock argued that once Treasury Secretary Henry Paulson announced that the federal government's primary role would be to support Fannie Mae and Freddie Mac and the $5 trillion in debt and guarantees associated with them, it signaled a green light for buying shares of Annaly and other M-REITs. Few investors were paying attention to this. In September, when these agencies were placed into conservatorship, federal backing of the mortgage agencies effectively went from being an implicit guarantee to an explicit guarantee. This made companies like Annaly Mortgage extremely safe investments despite dividend yields in the 15 percent range.

At the time, Krebs was so shaken by the market meltdown that safety was the only theme he could settle on for his portfolio. Annaly's relatively safe 15 percent yield sounded good to him.

"There wasn't much difference between putting your money in T-Bills and putting them in M-REITs because these companies could liquidate their portfolios and sell them to Fannie and Freddie, who were using money from the federal government to buy them," says Krebs.

So in mid-2009 after Annaly shares had bottomed and were on the way up from their low of $12, Krebs began buying shares. Annaly's stock was selling for below its book value. As the market and Annaly's stock price rose, Krebs began to sell put options "underneath" the stock.

Says Krebs, "I was in a position that if these options were exercised and the stock was actually put to me, 25 percent of my net worth would have been in that one stock. But I had determined that the stock was already below book value, so I would have been getting the stock at a very deep discount."

The put options Krebs sold were never exercised, so he was able to keep his premium income and earn healthy dividends on the shares he owned.

"I purchased the stock over a long period, and at one point I had nearly 10 percent of my portfolio in Annaly," says Krebs. Ultimately Annaly's stock rallied through the summer and fall, climbing to $16 and then $18. Krebs then decided to start writing out-of-the-money covered calls at strike prices of $19 and $20, well above the stock's market price. This effectively hedged his profits and locked in gains of nearly 50 percent, excluding his 15 percent dividend yield and the premium income he got writing puts and calls.

"Taken all together I think I generated $15 in gains on a stock that I had an average cost of $13 on. I think if you add in my premium income and dividends, I made close to 150 percent on Annaly in 2009," says Krebs.

Thus Krebs took what was otherwise a mundane, but high-yielding, M-REIT and magnified his income from this one holding by selling options against it. It's this kind of opportunistic options selling that helped Krebs end 2009 with an overall portfolio return of 25 percent—despite the fact that he held more than 50 percent of his assets in cash for the entire year.

Strategy Tip

Investors have long been advised by the financial press that falling stocks create the best bargains, and some are tempted to buy more stock as the price falls. Krebs warns against *doubling down* and almost always buys into rising stocks. He says trying to catch falling knives is best left to hedge funds and other professional investors.

Krebs
In His Own Words

On Avoiding the Big Loss

A while ago I read an article about 50 journeyman cabinetmakers and how some had more than 30 years of working around table saws, shapers, band saws, routers, etc. and had actually managed to still have all their fingers intact. Most however, had lost a digit or had other work-related accidents. What was the secret to their ability to avoid the Big Loss?

The authors interviewed about 40 of the accident victims who almost to a man stated that they *knew* just before the accident that they were at undue risk. Their primal safety sensors in their brain were screaming *"Stop!"* but their "intellect" overrode the warnings, and each man continued with his task resulting in an accident. So what was different about the 10 men who did not lose a finger?

The journeymen who still had all their fingers intact said that they *always* listened to that primal little voice screaming "Stop!" When they heard it, they would step away from their equipment, and take a break. They would think about where the potential hazard was and then set up the machinery for more safe operation until they felt they had reduced the risk to an acceptable level. Also, they did not operate the equipment when too tired, would not be rushed, and never ran equipment after drinking.

I was particularly intrigued by one 85-year-old gentlemen who had worked around these potentially maiming machines without serious accident for more than 70 years who related a practice that I now use each time I go into my workshop. It may seem too simple or a little silly, but it works.

Before this journeyman would begin his job, he would inspect his hands for about three or four minutes. That's right, he would hold out his hands and really *look* and *feel* how they were wondrously made. He would wiggle the digits and look at where the thumb was in relation to the fingers, he would flex and marvel at their agility. He would know to a millimeter exactly how large each part of his hands were. He would try to imagine what it would be like to be without any part of his hands. Then he would start work. His extremely intimate knowledge and high regard for his hands kept him from making careless mistakes with them.

I think we can apply some of these ideas to investing and avoiding the Big Loss.

The Big Loss is one from which you cannot easily recover.

Most investors on ValueForum have a nest egg that they have been building on for years, and they work hard trying to make it grow. The one thing that is generally unacceptable is to incur a Big Loss that will take years of work to recover. Most of us are not in a position to begin building that nest egg from scratch or even building one-half to one-third of that nest egg over again. Most of us can with reasonable risk expect to return 10–20 percent in good market years, but in search of extraordinary gains (30–60 percent) we are usually putting ourselves in a position for a potential Big Loss.

Like the old journeyman, we need to take time to look at our investments and our budget situations often and wonder what it would be like to lose a large portion of it. We should objectively look at each investment and determine if under some extraordinary circumstance a Big Loss could occur. This is especially true using options, margin, and leverage.

Look at each investment and listen for that little voice that says, "I have taken much too much risk here with too much of my money." If you hear it, do not then override it with your analytical intellect that says, "It's okay. I have looked at all the charts and the data and the analysts' expectations, I 'know' it could not possibly result in a Big Loss." Especially if you have been on a long winning run and your pride has convinced you there is no problem. Heed the little voice and take some risk off the table. Step away from the whirring saw blades of the market and take a break.

—August 2008, ValueForum.com

A Silver Lining to the Crash of 2008

It was a disastrous year from nearly all viewpoints, except perhaps one . . .

I have long been concerned that the rampant consumerism and (let's call it what it is . . . greed) has launched us (myself included) into a stratosphere flowing with giddy enthusiasm and unreasonable expectations of entitlement.

I need a new car because mine is no longer stylish; I need a new flat screen because my old one is only a 40-inch and not HD; I am expecting my house to appreciate at least 10 percent again this year; I am projecting 20 percent returns on my portfolio for the next 20 years that will provide a nice retirement . . . I need my daily White Mocha Frappuccino Grande with whipped cream (translated, 16 oz. premade coffee with some white mocha syrup and a little whipped cream on top, about $5! Really at that price, you should be sitting in a movie theater) . . . the list goes on and on.

If this vicious recession has a silver lining at all, it might be that as we struggle through it and come out the other side we will get back to simpler and more profound ways to reach fulfillment:

Loving times with family and friends
Sharing and giving to one another
Finding some good books to read and share
Strengthening our faith and helping others
Investing our time into our children
Stop wasting our resources (time, talent, money) on meaningless things
Spending more time with people and less with the LCD monitor
Inviting the neighbor over for dinner, instead of envying his new car
—*December 31, 2008, ValueForum.com*

CHAPTER

Lady's Man

Investor: Mike Koza

Date of Birth: April 10, 1959

Hometown: Sacramento, CA

Personal Web Site: None

Employment: Civil engineer, waste management and recycling

Passions/Pursuits: Whitewater rafting, ballroom dancing

Investment Strategy: Turnarounds and other special situations

Brokerage Accounts: Scottrade

Key Strategy Metric: Intrinsic value

Online Haunts: www.marketocracy.com, www.yahoo.com/finance, www.google.com/finance, www.investorshub.com

Best Pick: Radian Group, Up 1,200 percent

Worst Pick: ChipMos Technologies, Down 92 percent

Performance Since February 2001: Average annual return 34 percent versus 1 percent for S&P 500[1]

Y ou may have heard the old saying that behind every great man there is a great woman. In the case of armchair guru Michael Koza, the saying fits like a glove. If not for his mid-life marriage to Filipina wife Maria, Koza may have never realized his potential as an investor. Nor would the Kozas have become multimillionaires within the span of a decade. Marrying Maria changed Mike Koza's financial life.

In 2001, it was Maria who urged her new husband to dump his broker at Morgan Stanley and begin investing on his own. Koza was content working his civil engineering job for the government and spending weekends in the central California countryside whitewater rafting and otherwise enjoying the outdoors. "I wasn't into money," says Koza. "My wife said to me, you are smart in math, why don't you start investing on your own."

The rest is history. According to Marketocracy.com, which has been tracking Mike Koza's returns since February 2001, he has turned his $1 million virtual Torrid Growth Fund portfolio (TGF) into nearly $14.6 million, producing an average annual return in excess

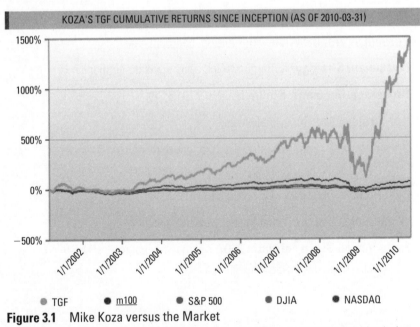

Figure 3.1   Mike Koza versus the Market

Note: Returns are after all implied fees including 5c/share transaction fees; SEC fees; management and administration fees of 1.95 percent.

Source: Marketocracy.com; data as of March 31, 2010.

of 34 percent for the last nine years versus about 1 percent for the S&P 500 (see Figure 3.1.)

Koza, it seems, has a knack for identifying turnaround stocks. With nerves of steel and a clear vision of a company's long-term prospects, Koza buys when others are panicking or otherwise over-reacting to bad news.

But his impressive returns are not just virtual; according to Koza, his Marketocracy portfolio is just a proxy for his real-life bro-kerage account. In fact, he says he has turned his $100,000 nest egg into a stock portfolio worth more than $3 million. This, despite suffering through a 50 percent portfolio decline in 2008, and with-drawing hundreds of thousands in cash to buy a new house, as well as several rental properties and, of course, to pay income taxes.

Knife Catching

Mike Koza's journey to stock picking superstardom has not been without bumps. When he first started investing in 2001, Koza admits to being sucked into a number of value traps. A value trap can occur when a stock has dropped in price and then appears to be a great bargain as measured by the classic value investing metrics of price-to-book value (P/BV), dividend yield and price earnings ratio (P/E).

Investors often get lured into these stocks selling at single-digit P/Es or P/BVs below one, or sporting high yields, but these stocks never rebound or appreciate to a more normal level. Sometimes they even fall further.

During 2007, and even 2008, many investors piled into financial stocks like Washington Mutual because they threw off great divi-dend yields and were arguably undervalued. Most were wiped out when the bank experienced a run on deposits in 2008. Washington Mutual's mortgage-laden portfolio was its undoing. A number of very smart value investors like *Forbes* columnist and contrarian David Dreman got stung badly by Washington Mutual.[2]

Strategy Tip

Value traps are bargain stocks that never get out of the bargain basement. Oftentimes they sink lower. Determining the difference between a truly undervalued stock and a value trap is the key to successful contrarian investing.

"I did some low price-to-book screens," says Koza. "I bought Guilford Mills, which is a textile company that was going out of business in the U.S., and another company called U.S. Aggregates. They both had very high book values relative to their stock prices, but they weren't really worth anything. So, I learned that the hard way."

In his hunt for value stocks Koza also bought into outright scam stocks including Worldcom, an international shipping fraud called ACLN and Actrade Financial, an e-commerce company that went into bankruptcy, leaving a wake of lawsuits.

"They were all low P/E stocks. I learned that you have to be careful with low P/Es, and find out why they are cheap," says Koza. Eventually Koza decided to focus on stocks that had fallen significantly, but that had some special circumstance surrounding the decline. One example is when a company issues shares in connection with a secondary stock offering. More shares outstanding means dilution, and this depresses stock prices. Oftentimes, it's only temporary.

Mike Koza has developed a keen sense for determining which stocks are turnaround plays and separating them from the value traps. He is typically a bad news buyer. This ability to catch a falling knife is a skill that few on Wall Street accomplish successfully.

"I prefer that stocks have short-term headwinds depressing the price," says Koza, who says low multiples of enterprise value to adjusted earnings is what he looks for.

The market crash of 2008 created an ideal environment for Koza's turnaround strategy. He was down more than 50 percent that year, but the following year his Marketocracy portfolio had a total return of 249 percent. In fact, Koza's heaviest buying months occurred in the first quarter of 2009 as stocks were plummeting globally.

One example of this is Trina Solar Limited (NYSE: TSL), a Chinese maker of photovoltaic solar panels with American Depository Shares trading on the NYSE. Koza first started buying the stock in late 2007 but really made a killing in 2008 and 2009 after its stock fell from a split-adjusted $25 per share down to less than $4 per share (see Figure 3.2).

"During the financial crisis none of the solar companies were making money because you have to get financing to install solar panels. The banks stopped financing them," says Koza. "Their other

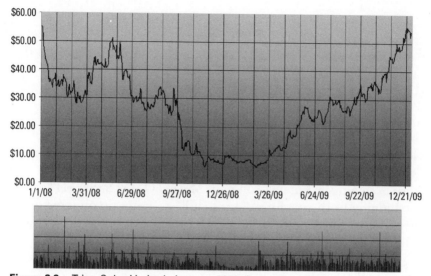

Figure 3.2   Trina Solar Limited, January 2008–December 2009
Source: © TickerTech.com, 2010.

problem was that they are in a commodity-type business, so prices went through the floor. As solar prices dropped, they took inventory losses." Indeed, Claymore's newly minted Global Solar Energy Index ETF (NYSE: TAN) plummeted 80 percent from June 2008 through March 2009.

However, Koza knew that Trina was one of the premiere manufacturers of solar panels, and his analysis of its books convinced him that its operations were sound. He also took comfort in its modest net debt levels. He reasoned that once the tight credit and panic selling passed, the supply imbalance in the solar panels would give way to a rapid increase in demand for them.

During the second half of 2008, Koza scooped up more than 25,000 shares as its share price went down from $20 per share (split adjusted) to $15, down to $10 per share and then bottoming at less than $4 per share.

Most of Koza's buying occurred at about $6 per share. Koza's cool analysis of Trina was vindicated as it reported strong earnings growth per share in the first half of 2009. By January 2010, its stock had rebounded to as high as $30. Koza began taking profits as the stock rose from $20 to $30 and still owned shares as of March 2010.

Strategy Tip

Management earnings calls are freely available on company web sites, Yahoo Finance, and Google Finance. Koza burns them to CDs and listens to them in his car.

Other "falling knives" that Koza has skillfully profited from include Genworth Financial (NYSE: GNW), mortgage insurer Radian Group (NYSE: RDN), Hartford Financial Services Group (NYSE: HIG), and Russian mining and metals company Mechel OAO (NYSE: MTL).

Judging by the copious notes that Koza writes up on most of his investments and the hours he spends in his car listening to earnings calls, it's clear that self-taught investor Koza puts his portfolio holdings to the same rigors that you would expect from the best Wall Street analysts.

Integral to Koza's analysis is his calculation of a company's intrinsic value, which, in his view, is the present value of the cash flow that a company does not need to run its business.

He calculates intrinsic value by first coming up with an adjusted forward earnings estimate and then applying a conservative multiple. He typically applies 6 for slower-growing companies and 10 for faster growers.

Unlike most value investors, Koza does not generally add back depreciation and amortization expenses to calculate cash flow because he believes that money is not available to shareholders if the company is to continue operations.

However, Koza says that when there is amortization of goodwill or intangibles related to an acquisition he will add them back into earnings because he isn't convinced that those expenses are truly needed to run the business. He will subtract out taxes at the appropriate rate because those are real and mostly unavoidable.

Koza says he will also tweak his intrinsic value calculation adding to it "excess cash" or cash not necessary to run the business or pay debt. Other things he will use to adjust his intrinsic value calculation include tax credits, net operating loss carryforwards, and real estate.

For financial companies, which Koza invested heavily in during the financial stock meltdown, he typically calculates book value and then subtracts out intangibles like goodwill. For distressed financials he will often apply a discount factor to intrinsic value to compensate for the time he figures it will take for the company to return to normalized earnings.

Koza generally avoids companies with excessive debt, but does not shy away from troubled companies. "I will buy only if I think they are not going bankrupt," says Koza.

Like others profiled in this book (and many professional investors including hedge fund great, Seth Klarman of The Baupost Group) Koza says special situations are his ideal candidates.[3] "I like short-term disconnects in the market," he says, pointing to occurrences like index fund rebalancing, warrant expiration/forced redemptions, and the misinterpretation of news events. Koza also likes stocks that are being neglected by Wall Street.

"Special situations add a degree of safety to my intrinsic value approach," he says. "Even if I am incorrect in my valuation, the special situation may cause the stock price to rebound."

Koza's eclectic value approach adheres to no one discipline though he does admit that early in his investing education he read most of Benjamin Graham's classic investment book *The Intelligent Investor*. He also read with interest Peter Lynch's two books *Beating The Street* and *One Up on Wall Street*. Another guru Koza admires is James P. O'Shaughnessy, author of *What Works on Wall Street*, which combines growth, value, and a bit of momentum using price-to-sales ratios, dividend yields, and relative strength.

How does Koza come up with ideas? Like many other great investors Koza is a voracious reader of news and information online. He devours financial documents including 10-K annual reports, 10-Q quarterly reports, and proxy statements. He spends at least four hours per day on the Internet. This includes an hour or so during lunch when he drives to his former residence, now vacant, where he keeps a Web-connected computer.

Additionally, Koza gets ideas from networking online. He regularly scans the day's top gainers and losers to look for companies where he thinks there may be market overreaction or misinterpretation going on.

Koza tried stock screeners several years ago but gave up on them. He also gives no weight to technical analysis.

Koza says that many of his ideas come naturally during research. "Once I get into one stock in the industry, I look at all the other stocks in the industry, and often I'll find one that's better," says

Koza. "A lot of times people on the boards will mention other companies." Koza earned big profits in Trina Solar, for example, but he also found out about another of his portfolio winners, Canadian Solar (NASDAQ: CSIQ) while researching Trina.

Koza's wife Maria subscribes to one investment newsletter that focuses on Chinese stocks, and they both occasionally attend free investor conferences like the Money Show. One stock Koza's wife urged him to buy was Allos Therapeutics (NASDAQ: ALTH), a biopharmaceutical company that develops cancer drugs. Koza's wife had heard about the stock on PBS's *Nightly Business Report.* Koza wisely listened to his wife, and they made a small profit in the stock.

One stock Maria told her husband about but he ignored was Human Genome Sciences (NASDAQ: HGSI). Maria says she gave her husband the tip when its stock was trading at $0.50 during early 2009. Mike never bought its shares, and it ran up to more than $30 a year later. Maria has not let Mike forget that "miss." "It will always be in my dreams," says Maria.

Koza typically holds 40 stocks and makes from 20 to 40 trades per month. His portfolio turnover averaged around 35 percent per quarter in 2009.

In terms of sectors, Koza will venture almost anywhere and has a significant number of small- and micro-cap stocks in his portfolio. As a rule, he tries never to go above 12 percent for any one position. He adds that any stock that represents more than 10 percent of his portfolio must have an intrinsic value that is three times its current share price.

Koza's sell discipline is tied into his intrinsic value calculation for each stock. If his intrinsic value figure divided by the current share price goes below 1.25, he sells.

Who Is Mike Koza?

Mike Koza was born in 1959 and was raised in Sacramento, California. He graduated from California Institute of Technology in Pasadena, CA, in 1981 with a degree in mechanical engineering. After Caltech, Koza went to work in the aerospace business for the Douglas Aircraft division of McDonnell Douglas. Today Koza is a civil engineer who works for the Sacramento County Department of Waste Management and Recycling.

However, when you start probing Koza about his life and career, you soon realize Mike Koza's life didn't really begin until he was 40 years old in 1999. That is when he met Maria.

Five feet eleven inches tall, brown hair with sunken green eyes and an admitted lack of assertiveness, Koza comes off a bit like a nerdy Jimmy Stewart.

Corporate ladders and money were never his thing. He was content collecting his modest salary working in environmental remediation. Mike was proud that his job helped clean up California's land and water. In fact, he took a pay cut when he left the aerospace business in 1989 to move back to Sacramento. He preferred cleaning up the environment to designing aircraft and wanted to be closer to the great outdoors of north central California.

About the only thing that Koza was passionate about was whitewater rafting. So on weekends and for vacations, he would head to rivers like the South Fork American River, east of Sacramento and west of Lake Tahoe, Nevada. Occasionally he and a friend would guide other groups through the rapids. "I like to take risks," admits Koza of his whitewater trips. "I have done some of the more dangerous rivers in this state, a lot of nasty stuff."

But by age 40, something was missing. Koza wanted to find a mate. So Koza picked up the *Sacramento Bee* and found Maria Adres in the personals ads.

Their first date was the clincher. "He took me to Olive Garden for dinner. And then, at the end of the meal, he left a small portion and took it home in a doggie bag," says Maria, who is a year older than her husband. "That's how I noticed that this guy has potential in life."

She adds, "Many of the men I met had maybe 10 credit cards in their pocket, but to me that was not a good sign."

Maria Koza is a Filipina immigrant. Her life story is one of poverty and hardship. She is originally from the small town of Guinayangan, in the province of Quezon, about six hours southeast of Manila.

At age 23, after completing nursing school in Manila, Maria became pregnant but before the baby was even born, its father took off.

"I had to leave my baby, leave my mother to find greener pastures," says Maria explaining that she needed to go find work to support her family. Maria left Manila in 1983 when her daughter Rarity Rome was only 18 months old.

Maria traveled to the Middle East, working in Saudi Arabia and Oman for 10 years as a nurse, sending money back to her family in the Philippines. Eventually Maria came to live in California where her elderly father had settled. She wanted to see him during his final years.

However, Maria's nursing license wasn't transferable. Unable to find steady work Maria eventually began taking on odd jobs in order to survive. She toiled for years as an illegal alien in California.

"People were walking all over me," says Maria. "I worked for a surgeon taking care of his mentally disabled child. He did not pay me for six months because he knew that I was illegal and that I could not do anything to fight him."

As the years went on, Maria was eager to find an American husband. She wanted financial security, and she wanted a green card. Mike Koza seemed to be a perfect fit. He was smart, humble, and frugal. And the couple seemed to hit it off.

Mike enjoyed taking Maria ballroom dancing, and when he was around her he felt happy, often acting childishly. The couple dated for about a year and then in 2001 they drove down to Reno, Nevada (Maria doesn't like to fly) and got married.

While they were courting during the late 1999s and early 2000, Maria noticed that the professional advice Michael was getting from stockbrokers at Morgan Stanley was doing his portfolio little good.

"I had a full-service broker because I thought that was supposedly the way to go. I had about $100,000 saved. So, they put me in a lot of Morgan Stanley Dean Witter funds and an annuity, and they went down," says Koza. "Then this guy who sold me the annuity, he had me buy some stock, and it went down. Then, he quit his job and went back to work on a farm."

Despite her five-foot three-inch frame and faint, heavily accented voice, girlfriend Maria was not shy about giving her future husband advice.

"I was reading about the stock market, but I did not have a clue what it was all about," says Maria. "So I asked a friend who had been a mentor to me, and he told me that we could make 40 percent, as long as Michael knows what he is doing."

"When I told Michael this, he did not believe that we could make 40 percent a year." So I told him, "Well, you're mathematically bright," referring to Koza's Caltech engineering degree and

his high math SAT score. "I challenged him, 'Why don't you liquidate that account and start managing that money?'"

That is exactly what Mike Koza did, and while he has not yet
achieved 40 percent average annual returns, 34 percent per year
for nearly a decade is pretty impressive.

"I guess I've always been considered a smart cookie, though
I am mathematically dumb," says Maria. "But I'm very resourceful
and very observant. Having been from a poor country, my only gift
from God is common sense."

The Kozas now have a stock portfolio worth more than $3 million,
despite suffering 50 percent losses during 2008. They also own two
homes and rental properties. The Kozas are debt free except for a
small mortgage they maintain on their first home.

Quips Maria, "It's a team effort. I guess I am the visionary and
he is the doer."

Though the Kozas are wealthy, they live frugally. Maria is very
much in charge of all household spending. Mike goes to work,
manages their stock portfolio, and prepares the couple's tax return.

Last year, they purchased a new 2,200 square foot home in the
Arden section of Sacramento. They still maintain their former residence, a four-bedroom home in Rancho Cordova, which is run
down and filled with their belongings and items that Maria accumulated over the years. Mike uses this house during his lunch breaks
to research stocks and check on his portfolio.

The Kozas' new home has no television, and there is a single
laptop computer with broadband access that they share. After strug-
gling for months using an ancient printer they found abandoned,
Mike recently broke down and purchased a new $40 computer
printer from Wal-Mart. The couple makes telephone calls from
phones they picked up in rummage sales. One phone cost $1, and
the other was free.

"We are both cheap; before I met Maria, I didn't run the central heat in the winter. I put a space heater in my room," says Koza.
Adds Maria, "We live way, way below our means."

The Kozas like to visit rummage sales regularly, and Michael
spends many weekends driving his spouse around in their pickup
truck listening to recorded earnings calls while Maria sorts through
bins for bargains.

Much of the clothing and household items that Maria finds
these days she ships back to the Philippines in boxes destined

for impoverished members of her extended family. The couple recently sent $20,000 to Maria's brother in Manila who had had a heart attack and needed assistance with medical bills. The Kozas also regularly donate clothing to the Salvation Army and other local charities.

Though the couple appears to be very spiritual and live what is in some ways a monastic existence, the only time they ever go to church is when there is a rummage sale.

"My belief is God is everywhere," says Maria. "When I am gardening and when we are rummaging and buying stuff cheap, sometimes we get a lot of freebies and I believe that God is with us." She adds, "I'd rather spend time looking for stuff I can give to the needy than sitting in church."

The Kozas are a match made in heaven and by all accounts financially secure. Still, Michael has no intention of quitting his day job to be by his honey's side.

He remembers all too vividly the stress he felt from his number one portfolio client during the financial crisis and stock market meltdown.

"Every day, Maria would call me at work and be crying on the phone," he recalls. "And every morning she would wake me up at 6:00 a.m., whether I liked it or not, because she would run to the computer and turn it on (and check our portfolio). I would try and get out of the house before she got upset, because every morning she'd be upset."

According to Mike Koza getting out of the house leads to a healthier marriage and a healthier stock portfolio. "I don't need to work anymore, but I don't want to stay at home all day. You can stare at the market all day, but if you look at it too long, you will try to do too much, and you will overdo it."

Koza's Rules of Investing

- **Look for short-term market "disconnects."**

  Mike Koza loves special situation stocks. These are stocks where some unusual event is causing its stock to be mispriced. These include events like companies being dropped from market indexes or companies issuing shares causing dilution. Or as in the case of Trina Solar, Genworth, and Radian, fear overtaking rational pricing. Koza frequently reviews biggest

losers and gainers each day and investigates the causes of
their extreme price action.

- **Successful investing requires a major time commitment to
  stock research.**

  Many investors rely on tips from message boards or commentary from pundits like Jim Cramer to guide them in their
  investment decisions. But according to Mike Koza successful
  investing requires a lot more than gleaning tips from your
  favorite stock guru.

  If he takes a meaningful position in a stock, he has typically read through at least one year's worth of financial filings,
  including prospectuses and annual and quarterly reports. He
  also spends hours of his spare time listening to management
  conference calls that he has downloaded from the Web. Then
  Koza documents his thesis by writing up his research and
  analysis.

  Says Koza, "My hobbies have been cut to a bare minimum.
  I no longer watch television. I sleep with 10-Ks and 10-Qs
  under my pillow, and carry the *Wall Street Journal* in my back
  pocket."

- **Don't accept company figures when analyzing a stock.**

  Koza doesn't merely accept the income statement or
  balance sheet figures he culls from company financial statements. Like a master chef, Mike Koza adjusts the financial
  ingredients that go into his estimates for calculating intrinsic
  or fair value. In some cases, Generally Accepted Accounting
  Principles (GAAP) skew reported figures. In almost all cases
  Koza tries to be conservative in his financial adjustments.

- **Avoid value traps.**

  As an investor who likes to find bargains among distressed
  stocks that he thinks will turn around, Koza often hunts in a
  part of the market where so-called value traps are common.
  These are stocks selling at low P/Es or low price-to-book values that would have them appear to be screaming bargains.
  As Koza puts it, some stocks are cheap for a reason, and unless
  he can see a clear path to improved profitability, or some cata-
  lysts that will cause their prices to rise, he avoids them.

- **Sell when the ratio of intrinsic value to price falls below 1.25.**

  Like others profiled in this book Koza tries not to
  become emotionally attached to any one stock. If stocks in

his portfolio either appreciate greatly or deteriorate in his estimation of their value to the point where their intrinsic value-to-price ratio goes below 1.25, he sells.

However, if you examine Koza's trading records, it is not uncommon for him to revisit stocks he has researched before. In stocks like mortgage insurer Radian Group, Koza traded in and out of the stock many times with great success.

Case Study: Radian Group (NYSE: RDN)

Mike Koza's investment in Radian Group (see Figure 3.3) falls squarely in the category of "special situations." It is a classic example of Mike's contrarian approach to stock investing and his fearless buying in the face of investor panic.

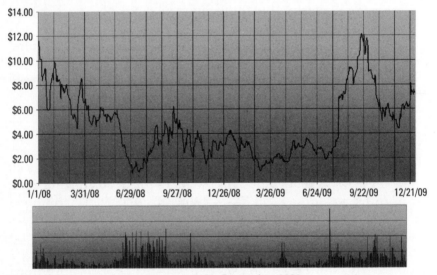

Figure 3.3   Radian Group, January 2008–December 2009
Source: © TickerTech.com, 2010.

NYSE-listed Radian Group is a Philadelphia-based mortgage insurance company. Radian was riding high during the housing boom. Indeed by the end of 2006 it had record earnings of $582 million or $7 per share and a reported book value of $51. For years its motto has been "Ensuring the American Dream."

However, during the housing bubble collapse and mortgage security meltdown of 2007 and 2008, the news reports coming out of Radian were the stuff of shareholder nightmares.

One of its joint ventures that specialize in buying subprime mortgages and securitization was hit hard causing it to report big losses. Moreover, mortgage insurer MGIC Investment (NYSE: MTG) backed out of a $5 billion deal to acquire Radian. By mid-2007 its stock had fallen from nearly $70 to the mid-teens.

Mike Koza first took an interest in the stock in September 2007 after he had read a story in *Barron's* detailing how renowned value investor Martin Whitman of Third Avenue Funds was buying the stock. The article reported how Whitman was initially a buyer of 2 percent of the company's outstanding shares at a price of around $60, but as the price had fallen to $14 or so he had doubled down on his investment and now owned more than 10 percent of its stock.[4]

Koza bought a small stake in Radian in late October 2007 when its stock was trading around $13. "I never really felt comfortable with it then because the housing market was still declining very rapidly," says Koza.

Koza started digging into its SEC filings, listening to conference calls, and reading through company presentations available on Radian's web site. Since Radian is a financial stock, his focus was mostly on determining what its intrinsic value was, as measured by its tangible book value per share.

In the summer of 2008 all hell was breaking out among financial stocks as the soundness of the global economy came into question. The culprit was toxic mortgages and related securities, a market that Radian was a player in. Radian's stock plummeted to less than a dollar per share.

"Radian is one of those companies that had been hated over the entire crisis," says Koza. "But I analyzed its financial reports, and the cushion against losses was so big even though they were losing money it was ridiculous for the stock to go under a dollar."

He adds, "They were losing maybe a dollar a quarter, but the delinquency trends were stabilizing. They had a book value of nearly $25."

Here is an excerpt from notes that Koza wrote about Radian on July 4, 2008.

> Only $36B of the $147B in mortgages "Insurance In Force" are covered by Radian. Of that $36B, $3.1B is subprime, and probably about half of that is covered by reinsurance, and another $400M is already reserved for. So if 100 percent of subprime borrowers default tomorrow (no more premiums paid) with zero cures and zero recovery to Radian,

Radian could book losses as high as:

($3.1B × 0.5 − $0.4B) × 0.62 = $710MM after tax, assuming 50 percent reinsurance

If 50 percent of Alt-A borrowers default with zero cures and zero recovery to Radian, Radian could book losses as high as:

($5.6B × 0.5 × 0.5 − $0.6B) × 0.62 = $500MM after tax, assuming 50 percent reinsurance . . .

. . . So you are looking at a book value of $35.14 − $8.90 − $6.20 = $20 for this dire scenario. But you may need to add back a few bucks if the Sherman option is exercised.

Feeling pretty confident about his $20-plus worst-case scenario book value analysis for Radian, Koza bought hundreds of thousands of shares of Radian at prices from $0.98 to $1.55 in the summer of 2008.

Koza also liked that the panicked Street wasn't giving Radian any credit for the fact that its guarantee business was mostly non-mortgage CDOs.

Says Koza, "A lot of these companies, they didn't diversify. Radian diversified, so its guarantee business was primarily non–housing related; its investment portfolio was municipal bonds, so there was some diversification there."

It didn't take long for Koza to be vindicated in his Radian purchase. He sold some shares when its stock rebounded sharply to more than $6 in September 2008. Then its stock traded down below $3 again at the end of that year and in early 2009. Koza bought more Radian stock. He finally sold out the majority of his holdings by the fall of 2009 when credit markets had stabilized and Radian's stock ran as high as $12 per share.

Koza
In His Own Words

On Comparing the Market to Whitewater Rafting

It goes up and down. You have to time it right. You have to go there when the flow is right. If it's too high, you wipe out. If it's too low or if the weather is bad, you get stuck. And there's been a lot of that. Sometimes it was too high, and we had to hike out of the river.

So, there are some parallels to the market, yeah. It's mainly the risk-taking aspect. I've learned to be able to take risk, and deal with it, and not be afraid of it when other people were. That's the way it is with the markets.

—Spring 2010

On Professional Money Management

These professional money managers—who have impressive backgrounds and studied finance in school and went to Wharton and stuff—can't beat the market! What have I got? Well, I'm just completely different.

I am not sure I'd want to be a professional mutual fund manager. One of the problems is, I mean, I don't know how it is to be exposed to your clients. My wife, you know, she's my client. And I know from her stressing that you've got clients that just want to sell at the bottom. And you have to hold all this cash in your account for redemptions, or you're forced to sell. It's tough being a mutual fund manager. I don't envy them.

—Spring 2010

The Sorcerer's Apprentice

Investor: Kai Petainen

Date of Birth: September 26, 1974

Hometown: Ann Arbor, MI

Personal Web Site: The World Between My Ears (www.kaipetainen.com)

Employment: Computer lab manager

Passions/Pursuits: National parks, photography, hot saunas

Investment Strategy: Eclectic mix of leading academic quantitative theories

Brokerage Accounts: E*Trade

Key Strategy Metric: The F-Score

Online Haunts: www.marketocracy.com, www.aaii.com, www.alphaseeker.com

Best Pick: EZCorp, Up 578 percent

Worst Pick: Healthtronics, Down 83 percent

Performance Since February 2003: Average annual return of 17 percent versus 7 percent for the S&P 500.[1]

In investing as with any other discipline, having a good teacher can make all the difference. Indeed, most of the greatest investors on Wall Street studied at the feet of other experts in the business. Warren Buffett of Berkshire Hathaway and Bill Ruane of the Sequoia Fund were understudies of Benjamin Graham, who was a finance professor at New York City's Columbia Business School.

Billionaire investor, Ken Fisher, had the benefit of working with and living under the same roof as father Philip Fisher, a renowned value investor who wrote the classic investment tome *Common Stocks and Uncommon Profits* in 1958. Today there is a whole generation of top hedge fund managers who were spawned from the ranks of Julian Robertson's highly successful Tiger hedge fund. They learned from the best, and now these hedge funds, commonly referred to as Tiger Cubs, are the ones to watch.

However, if you were to take a closer look at most of these great investors, you would find that most had a head start on the road to investing success. They either came from wealthy or well-connected families or were smart enough to get into a top-tier university. In almost every case there was some critical factor that made a big difference and helped them secure their spot at the foot of an investment master.

Kai Petainen's investment skill and success have come to him in a circuitous way. Petainen is the computer lab manager at University of Michigan's Ross School of Business. He is not wealthy, he has no MBA or CFA, and he has no formal training in investing. His successful investment style has been gleaned from soaking in what professors and graduate students are discussing at the lab he manages. It comes from working his 9-to-5 job helping business school students and professors with their projects, setting up computer stock screens, and using trading simulation software.

Petainen is a natural student with a thirst for knowledge and an affinity for statistics and data. Thus the quantitative strategies being explored by the young MBAs and undergraduates at the University of Michigan are right up his alley. You could call Petainen a self-taught quant.

What's a quant? In Wall Street parlance quants are mathematically minded traders who use computers and statistical modeling to exploit anomalies in the market. Their goal: Produce superior investment returns.

And that is exactly what Petainen has been doing for more than seven years. In some ways, Disney's Sorcerer's Apprentice in the movie *Fantasia* reminds me of Kai Petainen. Except instead of things running amok, Kai has himself become a master at applying leading academic theories from well-regarded professors to his own stock picking.

Of course, self-effacing Petainen would never pretend to compare himself to the investment greats or even to the professors he cribs screens from. Still, his investing record since early 2003 is so impressive that many highly paid money managers would surely rather have his stats.

In February and March 2003 Kai Petainen created nine virtual funds on Marketocracy.com. All but two, which happen to focus on diversified U.S. equities and global stocks, are sector funds. Every single virtual fund he manages has beaten its relevant benchmark over the last seven years. Kai's two best funds, one focusing on consumer staples and materials stocks, and the other devoted to energy and utility stocks, have gained 27 percent and 24 percent per year

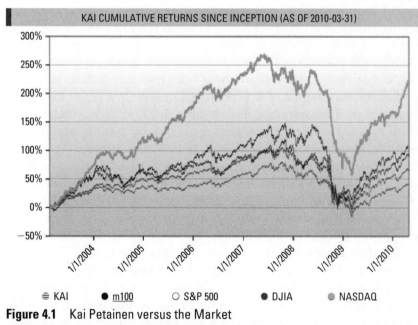

Figure 4.1   Kai Petainen versus the Market

Note: Returns are after all implied fees including 5c/share transaction fees; SEC fees; management and administration fees of 1.95 percent.

Source: Marketocracy.com; data as of March 31, 2010.

on average respectively since March 2003. This far outpaces their sector fund benchmarks and trounces the S&P 500, which gained about 6 percent over the same time period. Kai's diversified stock fund (KAI), shown in Figure 4.1, has had an average annual return of 17 percent since its inception in February 2003 versus 7 percent for the S&P 500. These returns are *after* deducting commissions and fees of $0.05 per share and a 1.95 percent annual management fee.[2]

Magpie Investing

A decade ago Kai Petainen didn't know what a P/E was; today he teaches young MBA students about capital markets, stock valuation, and portfolio management.

As a quant, he selects his investments based on statistical models that screen for various measurable attributes in companies and stocks. These models have determined that deviations in the values of some fundamental factors like low price-earnings multiples, are good predictors of alpha, which in investor-speak means, "beating risk-adjusted benchmarks." In other words, these quant models screen for stocks that will beat the market.

Petainen doesn't care much about reading annual reports, or kicking company tires or listening to management conference calls. He prefers hard cold data and fast screening software to impassioned pitches from analysts or CEOs.

"Sometimes people will ask me if I can give them a favorite stock, or what my best stock was and I can't remember," says Petainen. "They think that's strange, but I don't look at individual stocks. I look at baskets." Petainen's strategy is almost entirely based on a mix of leading academic theories on stock appreciation.

So if Petainen reads in a scholarly paper that low price-to-book ratio stocks tend to outperform over the long term, based on back testing, he will run computer screens analyzing SEC reported company stats to find stocks selling at a bargain relative to their book value or net worth.

Another perk of Petainen's job as computer trading lab manager for the University of Michigan's business school is his daily interaction with curious MBAs. He gets paid to help them with school assignments, and in doing so he is exposed to leading quantitative strategies. Indeed, Kai has become such an important resource for the MBA faculty that he now acts as a regular lecturer, teaching several portfolio management classes.

Several years ago Petainen helped Ross School accounting professor Richard Sloan conduct research for a study he was doing on how mounting accruals in a company's balance sheet were a tell-tale sign of ailing financial health. Ultimately it was a good predictor that a company's stock performance would suffer.

The landmark paper made a splash and eventually helped Sloan land a job as the managing director of equity research at banking giant Barclays Global. Sloan has since become a distinguished professor at U.C. Berkeley's Haas School of Management.

Sloan and his wife Patricia Dechow, group chair of Accounting at Haas, and others developed something called the F-Score, which measures more than two dozen variables and identifies companies likely to have material accounting misstatements. "F" stands for fudging or, as Kai puts it, "fraud." The F-Score uses an algorithm that compiles data on a company's sales, inventories, employee counts, receivables, and other factors and measures them against cash flow and assets.

Petainen was in on the ground floor of the development of the F-Score theory, and he and Sloan actually set up a web site called Earnings Torpedo (www.earningstorpedo.com) that identifies high F-Score candidates each month. These stocks are theoretically ripe for shorting. A low F-Score is one of 11 factors Petainen incorporates into his winning portfolio screens.

Another factor he uses is based on the theories of Joseph D. Piotroski, a former University of Chicago accounting professor who published *Value Investing: The Use of Historical Financial Statement Information to Separate Winners from Losers* in 2000. Kai discovered this paper on a well-known academic web site he trolls called Social Science Research Network, or SSRN.com.

Piotroski's paper talks of a nine-point scoring system for finding winning value stocks. One of Piotroski's most important factors is finding low price-to-book ratio stocks. However, given that many firms with low price-to-book ratios are often distressed, Piotroski also evaluates

Strategy Tip

Don't just look to popular investing sites for investment ideas and strategies. Kai Petainen trolls SSRN.com (Social Science Research Network), a virtual library of academic papers for new ideas. Google Scholar (http://scholar.google.com) is another resource.

balance sheet strength return on assets and cash flow. Buying those companies that passed Piotroski's rigorous test and shorting those that didn't would have produced a 23 percent average annual return for the two decades between 1976 and 1996. Petainen incorporates some of Piotroski's tests into his own quantitative formula.

Whenever Kai hears or reads about some new academic theory he thinks has potential, he test-drives it by back-testing it at the trading lab he manages. If he is impressed, he incorporates it in his stock selection formula.

I consider Kai Petainen to be a magpie investor. Like the birds that scavenge opportunistically and will eat just about anything once it realizes that it is edible, Kai's strategy ingests whatever theories he comes across that he thinks will work. After years of culling through academic research and running them through his simulations, Petainen has developed 11 variables he screens for before he buys stocks for his portfolios.

1. Low price-to-book value (Piotroski-inspired, less than 5)
2. Positive return on assets (Piotroski-inspired)
3. Positive return on equity (Piotroski-inspired)
4. Low debt-to-equity (generally less than 30 percent)
5. Relatively low price-earnings multiple
6. Price at or near its 52-week high
7. Five-year revenue growth rate of at least 10 percent but not more than 40 percent ("If revenue growth is too high, like 80 percent, I avoid it")
8. Low F-Score (including accrual formula, which is roughly equivalent to (net income – cash flow)/assets)
9. Low short interest
10. Institutional buying
11. Insider buying

Strategy Tip

Kai Petainen has access to expensive stock screening software called FactSet Research. Cheaper alternatives do exist. Google's finance site has a good free screener, and for a modest fee you can subscribe to StockScreen123.com or AAII's screening software, Stock Investor Pro.

One weekend every month, Petainen runs stock screens for his 11 attributes and comes up with a list of 50 stocks. He does this for all of his virtual sector portfolios on Marketocracy. Then he runs these stocks through two other checkpoints to whittle the list down to his 20 most eligible candidates.

One checkpoint is institutional stock evaluation software provided by The Applied Finance Group (AFG) (www.economicmargin .com), a Chicago-based research firm that specializes in intrinsic value analysis and market expectations. AFG is a subscription web site, but anyone can register to receive general economic and market analysis.

Petainen also checks with another Web tool called "eVal" that was created by his mentor Richard Sloan and another Michigan professor, Russell Lundholm, as a companion to their book *Equity Valuation and Analysis*. The book, including CD-ROM and password access to the eVal web site, costs $149 on Amazon.com.

Both of these services offer intrinsic value analysis, which provides Petainen with target prices for the stocks he is considering for his portfolio. If his portfolio candidates are deemed to be undervalued by these services, it confirms his thesis.

Once Petainen comes up with a list of 20 finalists, he allocates them to his portfolios. His goal is to have a portfolio of stocks that is roughly equal in weighting. Most of his portfolios have about 30 stocks in them.

In terms of market capitalization, Petainen only requires that stocks have at least $20 million in market capitalization and sell for more than $2 per share. That means some of his stocks are tiny, though Marketocracy's software has liquidity rules and forces micro-cap buyers to place large orders over several days. Petainen's portfolios are fully invested at all times, and he will often augment them with ETFs if his screens deliver overweighting or underweighting in various sectors.

How does Petainen know when to dump a stock? If one of Petainen's stocks drops more than 20 percent in any given month he sells it. Conversely, if it goes up more than 10 percent and he has cash on hand he often buys more of the stock. You can look at this Petainen tactic as paying homage to the momentum strategies professed by those like William O'Neil. Buy winning stocks and shed losers. It can work even if you are a value investor.

If a stock drops off Petainen's top 50 list after any monthly screen, he sells it. If it falls into the bottom 30 Petainen will reduce its weighting in his portfolio. He adds to stocks in the top 20.

Of course, like any methodology, Petainen readily admits that screening isn't foolproof. In October 2009, as Apple's (NASDAQ: AAPL) stock climbed above $200 and Jim Cramer suggested that it would continue on to $300, Petainen conducted a workshop for students at the university demonstrating why Apple was overvalued. He also wrote a long analysis of Apple on SeekingAlpha.com arguing that the stock might be a good "short" and in his headline suggested it was worth $80 per share.

Petainen wrote about how Apple didn't fit most of the characteristics of a value stock. It has high P/E, high price-to-book value, and in validation of his thesis he showed that it wasn't owned by value stock mutual funds. Petainen went on to discuss all of the different academically inspired quantitative valuation models that he checked, which mostly concluded that Apple's was overvalued.

Theoretically speaking Petainen was right. But markets aren't known for their strict adherence to academic theory; they are about supply and demand. People, including Kai Petainen, love Apple's products, and the company has been an investor darling recently. Many people who own Apple's stock don't care about its lofty P/E. The stock still sells above $200.

Petainen isn't recanting his lecture remarks, but it's also interesting to note that Petainen's Apple short never made it to his winning Marketocracy portfolios.

Who Is Kai Petainen?

Kai Petainen is a self-described "geek-nerd." He was born and raised in Sault Ste. Marie, a city in Northern Ontario just across the St. Mary's River from a city by the same name in Michigan. It's also at the confluence of Lake Huron, Lake Superior, and Lake Michigan. "The Sault" is best known for its locks connecting Lake Superior to the lower Great Lakes.

Kai's parents are from Finland. His mother was a nurse and his father was a neon-glass blower for a local sign company. Kai's father's passion, however, was photography.

Tragedy struck the Petainen family when Kai's father Matti suddenly died of an aortic aneurysm while at work. Kai was only eight years old. His mother was left to raise the family.

"That moment changed something in my life, because as a kid I suddenly became aware of how short life could be," says Petainen. "It became important to me to a live life where I would treat others nicely and not take anything for granted."

Kai's father left him his photography equipment, including a pair of Hasselblad cameras that he cherished, and of course young Kai took to photography immediately.

"Here I was, a kid, running around with two Hasselblads and snapping pictures of the world. My dad laid the groundwork for me, a passion in my heart for the shortness of life, and a legacy of art in my world," says Petainen.

But Kai had another affinity. He was good with numbers. Indeed, Petainen's quantitative roots run deep. "When I was a boy I would keep statistics of G.I Joe comics—I had a bunch of them—and I would keep statistics as to how many characters there were, who died when, how many episodes," says Petainen. "I liked databases."

Eventually Kai attended Lake Superior State University just across the International Bridge in Michigan majoring in math and computer science. Neither of his parents had been involved in investing or the stock market, and Kai knew little of the workings of Wall Street before he arrived at University of Michigan's Ross School of Business in the late 1990s.

Ironically it wasn't finance at all that drew Kai south to Michigan. He followed a girlfriend there whom he eventually married. Unfortunately, Petainen's first marriage was brief, but he has remained in Ann Arbor living in an apartment with his second wife Naomi.

Kai has become a fixture at University of Michigan's Tozzi Electronic Business and Finance Center. He has been its manager for nearly 12 years. He credits his growing passion and skill in stock picking to Professor Sloan and to the University of Michigan's trading center.

Initially Petainen worked a help desk at the computer room of the business school. But soon after he began working, Sloan asked him to help the school come up with a list of the proper computer equipment for a new state-of-the-art learning lab.

With the help of a $3 million donation, Kai, Sloan and other faculty members eventually developed a 5,800-square-foot, state-of-the-art wireless facility that includes a financial analysis and trading-floor classroom, an electronic classroom and an E-lab seminar room. It is equipped with live financial data feeds—such as

Bloomberg, Barra, and FactSet—information services, research tools, and trading tools.

According to Petainen up to 1,000 students use the Tozzi trading center each week, and about 20 classes utilize the lab for homework assignments. Kai can often be found giving noncredit workshops on quantitative strategies, screening, and using FactSet software.

Given Petainen's relatively modest income, Petainen figured his best option for becoming a good investor and testing what he was learning at work was to set up virtual million-dollar portfolios on Marketocracy.com. So in early 2003 Petainen became a virtual portfolio manager.

Like many others on the web site, Kai was attracted to the possibility of eventually being paid to manage money. While Petainen's performance has been outstanding and he has several funds in the site's top ranks, Marketocracy's real mutual fund has failed to attract significant assets. Kai's small bonuses from Marketocracy have done little to change his financial picture.

Unlike Marketocracy manager Mike Koza (see Chapter 3), Kai has never accumulated enough capital in real life to have the confidence to apply his techniques to his own nest egg. He rarely invests real money and mostly sticks to mutual funds in his 401(k) and personal accounts. "I don't have a lot of money," admits Petainen, "And whatever extra I have, I prefer to spend on vacations with my wife."

Kai and his wife Naomi are somewhat extreme in their vacation choices. Each year they take off for a month or so on a quest to explore the national parks. "My goal is to visit and photograph every national park in North America," says Kai, who went on a California national park tour in the summer of 2010.

Two years ago the Petainens drove 18,000 miles on their summer vacation all the way up to Alaska and the Northwest Territories, traveling for up to 17 hours a day. They also hiked the Chilkoot Trail, which goes from Dyea, Alaska, to British Columbia.

Kai's adventures have included swimming in the Arctic Ocean, singing the national anthem at sunrise on Canada Day at Signal Hill in Newfoundland, and snapping photos on hikes in parks from the Everglades to the Great Smoky Mountains to Glacier National Park in Montana.

You can see photos of Kai's adventures on www.kaipetainen .com, a personal photography blog he maintains called "The World

Between My Ears." Says Kai of his photos, "Perhaps I'll get a few people to explore a new area, or get off their lazy asses and see something in the world."

Given Kai's Finnish roots, he has another passion outside of stock investing and nature photography. Petainen loves to *schvitz*. In other words, Petainen was raised to appreciate the virtues of saunas. In fact, whenever he travels he will seek out good saunas and if he does find one he routinely cranks the heat to above 100 Celsius (212°F). "Then I jump in the snow," says Kai. "I love saunas, but I love the true Finnish sauna. There is a Finnish proverb . . . in a sauna, treat it as if it's a church."

Petainen's Rules of Investing

- **Find stocks that have** *smart money, value, growth,* **and** *quality* **attributes.**

  Okay, this first rule essentially sums up Kai Petainen's whole approach, which is "quantified" by the 11 screening attributes listed earlier in this chapter. Put simply, if a stock passes most of these criteria, it is by definition a value stock with good growth and a strong balance sheet. Add to this some approximation of "smart money," which in this case is insider buying of institutional ownership, and you have a stock Kai wants to own.

  Here are two examples:

  In April 2003 Austin, Texas–based EZCorp (NASDAQ: EZPW) showed up on Kai's screen. At the time, the small, but growing, pawn shop operator had revenues in the $50 million range, its stock was hitting new highs, its return on equity had recently turned positive, and it had a price-to-book value of 0.4. The company's cash on hand had increased significantly, its debt-to-equity ratio was declining, and its F-Score was a low 0.4 (low accruals). EZCorp's price earnings multiple was 11.6.

  Petainen purchased shares at $3 and held on to the stock for nearly three years. By March 2006 its price had appreciated to $23, and Kai sold it. Its shares eventually split three-for-one.

  Another stock recently passing Petainen's magpie 11-point screen was Shuffle Master (NASDAQ: SHFL), a company that supplies the casino business around the world with automatic card shufflers and other electronic table games. Kai purchased Shuffle Master's beaten-down shares in March 2009 at $2 and still owns them a year later $8.

Says Kai, "I don't look at news, technical charting analysis, bid/ask spread, transaction costs, product quality, analyst research reports, taxes, risk, beta, political factors, or economic macro variables."

- **Avoid story stocks.**

   It is not that Kai Petainen is against great company stories or miraculous turnarounds or firms that make fabulous products. It's just that he wants to remain as clinical and unbiased in his approach to investing as possible. So like many other investors with a value investing bias, Petainen simply ignores stocks that get a lot of media attention or have a great story.

   "I think Crocs (NASDAQ: CROX) is a good example of a story stock. Here was a stock that rose quickly and was loved by the media and blogs. It seemed to me that it was trading like a technology or biotech stock. But they made plastic shoes! Poor valuation, crazy growth, high short interest, high insider selling. . . . Yet it shot up very high. It also dropped like a rock."

- **Develop a sell discipline and stick to it.**

   As a rule, Kai Petainen will typically sell any stock that drops more than 20 percent from his purchase price. He also has a strict discipline of selling any stock that doesn't make his top 50 screen.

   Kai does admit that this method doesn't always seem logical. Sometimes stocks fall off his top-50 list, and he sells them, and then a few months later they turn up among the top 20 of his screen (his buy list). He buys them back even if their share prices have not changed significantly. If one of his top picks drops 10 percent and it is still showing up on his screen, he sometimes buys more if he has cash available.

- **Don't follow the flavor of the moment investing style.**

   "During the Internet boom, high P/E stocks did well. After the bubble burst, low P/E stocks did well, and then a few years later they weren't performing so well," says Petainen. Many investors tend to latch on to whatever they think is working at the moment. While some technicians have limited success with this, Petainen thinks it can lead to portfolio disaster.

In 2008 when the market crashed, Petainen stuck to his guns, and his portfolio of undervalued low P/E stocks fell hard and fast. In 2008, Kai's diversified portfolio fell 42 percent. His global fund fell 41 percent.

"I had to ask myself, 'Should I change my strategy? Do I remove P/E from my analysis?' It was tempting to remove it. But, the recession hit and if you had followed the low P/E strategy, it worked well again. So I was thankful that I did not remove the P/E from my analysis." In 2009, Petainen's diversified portfolio had a total return of 41 percent, and his global fund gained 69 percent. Petainen's discipline and consistency have served him well.

- **Don't data mine excessively.**

Petainen is unashamed of his affinity for data and his lack of interest in the exciting stock stories that make headlines. He also has used back-testing extensively in developing his investment strategy. However, he warns novice investors about the dangers of adopting criteria or variables in screens just because they seem to work.

"You read about things like the Super Bowl Indicator, or the hemline indicator. They may work for a selected period, but they don't make sense to me so I avoid them," says Petainen. (The Super Bowl Indicator says that if a football team from the old AFL [AFC today] wins the Super Bowl the market will decline during that same year, vice versa for an NFC win.[3])

In a sense Petainen's rule is a knock on some of the widely followed theories of technical analysis. Chartists look for specific patterns in price and volume that typically repeat themselves without much concern for the fundamentals that might cause them. Petainen gives little credence to these approaches.

Case Study: Ternium, S.A. (NYSE:TX)

Ternium is an example of a stock that has made Petainen's top 20 list several times. He first discovered Ternium in August 2006, when its NYSE-listed ADRs were selling for $25 per share (see Figure 4.2). Ternium is a big distributor of steel, especially in Mexico and Argentina. After doing his monthly screen for his

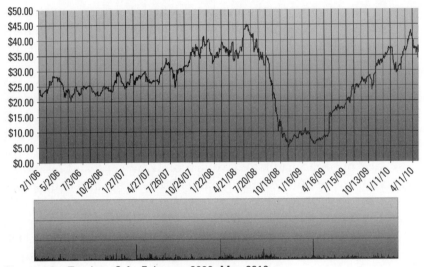

Figure 4.2   Ternium, S.A., February 2006–May 2010

Source: © TickerTech.com, 2010.

11 criteria, Ternium showed some very promising fundamentals. It had a price-to-book value of 1.6, its price earnings multiple was 6, it had a low "F" or fraud score of less than 1, and it seemed to measure up on all of Kai's criteria except for its sales growth, which was a bit high at 170 percent.

Kai decided to overlook that one measure and began buying the stock at $25 per share in August. He continued to buy it for nine months at prices up to $31. In January 2008, the trading records indicate that Petainen sold his shares for $34 when the stock dropped off his screen, either because its fundamentals deteriorated or because more attractive stocks replaced it among the top 50.

Ternium shares peaked at nearly $45 in mid-2008 but then plummeted to $5 per share during the financial meltdown that year. In January 2009, Ternium appeared on the screen Petainen prepares each month for his materials and consumer staples fund. Its price-to-book value was now about 0.37 percent, and its price earnings multiple was less than 3. Its return on equity was 19 percent. Of course Ternium was not selling anywhere near its high, but then again in January 2009, not many stocks were.

So Petainen bought shares at $8, but then only two months later it had fallen to $6 violating Petainen's 20-percent rule, so he sold most of his holdings. Less than two months later Ternium passed Petainen's screens again, and he purchased shares at $8 per share. He still held the stock nearly a year later when Ternium's shares were selling for $37 per share.

Petainen
In His Own Words

On Jim Cramer, John Stewart, Stock Analysts, and "Sisu"

By now everyone has probably heard about the Cramer/Stewart fiasco, and I have a few thoughts to add. Analysts are wrong, analysts are right, and although it is okay to call out an analyst when he is wrong, I think it wasn't completely fair that Stewart nailed Cramer. I love watching both of their shows. I had the privilege to see Stewart live in Detroit, and I've had the privilege to meet up with Cramer in person. Both are entertainers, and both try to educate their viewers. It should be noted that analysts make mistakes, but it should also be noted that some analysts just don't have the guts to give sell recommendations. Perhaps it's not the "sell recommendation" that people should look for, but the number of analysts that suddenly stop covering a company. So Cramer will make some good calls, and he will make some bad calls—don't expect him to be perfect. But at least he takes a stand. I do expect stock analysts to practice better stewardship, think outside the box, create true critical commentary of stocks, and develop some . . . errr . . . *sisu* or "strength of will," as the Finnish would call it.

—March 2009

CHAPTER **5**

Network Miner

Investor: Alan T. Hill

Date of Birth: May 11, 1939

Hometown: Placitas, New Mexico

Personal Web Site: None

Employment: Retired, educational-software executive

Passions/Pursuits: Baking bread, sports cars, his grandkids

Investment Strategy: Micro-caps and yield-oriented stocks

Brokerage Accounts: TD Ameritrade

Key Strategy Metric: Relative P/E

Online Haunts: www.valueforum.com, www.investorshub.com, www.investorvillage.com

Best Pick: China Energy, Up 670 percent

Worst Pick: China Shoe Co., Down 96 percent

Performance Since July 2005: Cumulative return of 1,026 percent return versus 28 percent for the S&P 500[1]

Like many of the other successful investors in this book, Alan T. Hill takes pride in the fact that he is prudent in the way he spends his money. In fact Hill is quick to point out that his parents lived through the Great Depression of the 1930s and that they raised him with the kind of values people of this era instilled in their offspring. So like his father Hill, 71, has never purchased a new car in his entire life.

"A new car depreciates something like 25 percent the first year," he says. "It just never made any sense to me. So I have two cars." Hill then goes on to mention his 1993 Toyota pickup truck, and his 2008 Toyota Scion. "The Scion gets 40 miles to the gallon!" he boasts.

However, Hill has another automobile tucked away in his garage that he's a bit embarrassed to talk about. It's a racing red 2002 Audi Roadster TT; a real cherry. But true to form Hill got it for a bargain on eBay in 2004 with only 4,000 miles on the odometer. "It's my toy," he says.

People sometimes say that the type of vehicle a man drives tells you a lot about his personality. In Hill's case it also gives you some insight into his very successful investment style. Alan Hill is an outstanding investor because he has been able to successfully blend what he calls "Steady-Eddy" conservative yield-oriented picks with high-risk, high-octane microcap stocks—kind of like owning a reliable Toyota and a flashy road racer at the same time.

According to the online stock community ValueForum.com, Hill's "buy" and "strong buy" recommendations have experienced an average return of 129 percent and 71 percent respectively, since he started posting recommendations in August 2004. Hill also participates in the web site's stock-picking contests nearly every quarter. Had you followed Hill's contest picks on ValueForum.com dating back to July 2005 you would have turned $10,000 into $112,600 versus a mere $12,800 for similarly timed investments in the S&P 500 (see Figure 5.1). That's a 1,026 percent cumulative return versus 28 percent for the S&P.[2]

Even more impressive than his Web record is what investor Alan Hill has accomplished in his real life. About a decade ago Hill invested in a single stock, the ADR for Colombia's Bancolombia (NYSE: CIB), and was able to make enough profit from it to build a retirement dream home in the scenic hills of Placitas, New Mexico. But rather than it being a single lucky hit, Hill is making more money now as an investor than he did during his working years.

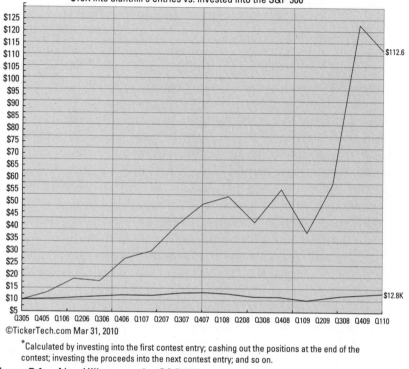

©TickerTech.com Mar 31, 2010

*Calculated by investing into the first contest entry; cashing out the positions at the end of the contest; investing the proceeds into the next contest entry; and so on.

Figure 5.1 Alan Hill versus the S&P 500

Source: ValueForum.com; data as of March 31, 2010, alanthill = Alan T. Hill's screename on ValueForum.com.

He's proving that enhancing an otherwise staid portfolio with little red sports cars can produce game changing returns.

Peer-to-Peer Profits

Ever since the Internet boom began, there has been a lot of excitement in Silicon Valley and other parts of the wired world about peer-to-peer investing. I know this because I covered the topic in *Forbes* for more than a decade. The idea really started back in what I call the Wild West of the Internet boom in the late 1990s, when people were opening up E*Trade accounts and getting rich from stock-trading ideas gleaned from message boards like Silicon Investor, Raging Bull, and Yahoo Finance.

This online trading mania occurred at roughly the same time that online music file-sharing site Napster was beginning to make headlines because it was disrupting the music business. Why not a "Napster" for investors, peer-to-peer networks where everyone would share ideas and become better, self-directed investors.

Eventually a slew of Web services were created to capitalize on the new "social networking" and investing phenomena, including Motley Fool Caps, Social Picks, BullPoo (now called Duedee.com), Vestopia, Covestor, and Cake Financial. Unfortunately, as business models go, few of these have made any significant traction.

Cake Financial is a good example of social investing gone awry. The San Francisco–based firm had the brilliant idea of getting people to link their real-life brokerage account trading records to their profiles on a Web service named Cake. The hope was that each member would build a trusted network of family, friends, and others, who would alert each other to buys, sells, and holds, and of course blog their stock ideas and insights. There was even a "Match Me Up" service so that you could find others with similar investment goals.[3]

Its CEO and founder Steve Carpenter would spend his time rallying the members, writing snarky blog posts, and recording cheeky video segments ("The Slice") about the market and the evils of established financial firms and how fun Web-connected, peer-to-peer investing could be. He urged everyday people to tap into the collective wisdom of Cake. Actually making a profit at Cake Financial wasn't the top priority.

Apparently Carpenter's plan sounded better on the PowerPoint he presented to venture capitalists (VCs) than it did to individual investors. By 2009 Cake scrapped its social investing model for one that used academic theories to offer asset allocation advice on mutual funds and 401(k)s.

Brokerage firm E*Trade finally put Cake out of its misery in early 2010 by purchasing the company for its user-friendly software and shutting it down.[4] So much for collective wisdom and peer-to-peer investing.

However, I believe that peer-to-peer investing *does* work. Only it doesn't work in a way that Silicon Valley VCs can easily package into neat digital business models. Retiree Alan Hill is living proof that peer-to-peer online investing works.

Hill is a member of three Web communities that he mines daily for investing ideas in an effort to improve his alpha. They are ValueForum.com, InvestorsHub.com, and InvestorVillage.com.

After his morning swim at his local gym, Hill spends more than four hours each day after the market opens in New York trolling the message boards on these sites for information and ideas. Alan has become skilled at separating the wheat from the message board chaff.

"Although I have a background in finance and possess an MBA, I do not consider myself a competent stock analyst," admits Hill. "What I think I do well is listen. Over time it becomes pretty apparent who the stock pumpers and blowhards are as opposed to the serious knowledgeable investors who are willing to share their expertise."

Before Hill starts seriously sifting through the boards, he develops his macro themes, mostly culled from Web research and forum postings from other investors he respects. "I kind of go where the money and the growth are," he says.

In 2005, about the time he was settling into his newly built 3,200-square-foot, pueblo-style house in New Mexico, Hill determined that energy and metals, including gold, were good themes for his portfolio.

So he dug into the message boards at ValueForum.com where some of the smartest and highest-rated members were buzzing about Canadian royalty energy trusts with yields in excess of 15 percent. They also were recommending mining stocks like HudBay Minerals (TSX: HBM), a Toronto-based zinc producer and Yamana Gold (NYSE: AUY), a gold-mining company with extensive interests in Brazil and other parts of Latin America.

Some of the best insights on gold mining came from "swannmex," a ValueForum member renowned for his insider-like expertise of gold mining (for more on swannmex, see Chapter 8). On ValueForum, Hill goes by the screen name "alanthill." "VikingFan," another member of the premium subscription site, tipped off Hill on the prospects for zinc. In this way Hill identifies smart people on each of the Web communities he belongs to. They help him gather research on stocks, and he helps them by posting the information he gathers tracking down stocks.

Strategy Tip

While "lurking" on message boards is common, Hill says that contributing good information is key if you want to make lasting connections to the other smart online investors. Hill's recommendations on ValueForum have improved his standing and expanded his network.

Once Hill gathers some insights from people on the forums that he trusts, he goes to work pulling SEC documents, visiting company web sites and generally reading as much as he can on his potential targets. A good deal of his time is spent corroborating information he has gotten from the postings he reads online. For example, Hill's research on zinc made him one of the community's most informed posters on the subject. Zinc, of course, is an anticorrosive used in galvanizing steel and other metals. The emerging markets boom had caused zinc prices to soar in 2005 and 2006.

Hill bet big on HudBay Minerals and Yamana Gold. In 2006 alone Yamana doubled in price. Hill says he started buying HudBay warrants in 2005 for $0.06 each and sold them at about $0.35 each by 2007.

When it comes to traditional stock valuation metrics, Hill keeps it simple. He wants growing revenues and earnings and a relatively low price-earnings multiple compared to peers.

Hill isn't immune from making costly errors. When playing among thinly traded stocks, often listed on foreign exchanges, volatility can be brutal. One of Hill's holdings, a Toronto gold-mining firm named Southwestern Resources, plummeted more than 85 percent in value after its CEO resigned amid scandal in 2007.[5] Indeed, in 2008 Hill's portfolio suffered along with most others, down some 40 percent.

"I don't have any hard-and-fast rules about selling. I need to get better about that. I usually sell too late," admits Hill.

These days Hill relies on the Web community at ValueForum .com for yield plays and more conservative stock picks. Like other ValueForum members, including Bob Krebs (see"dig4value" in Chapter 2), Hill took the advice of veteran ValueForum members like "Xstock" and "Bonddaddy," and has made a killing in mortgage REITs like Annaly Capital (NYSE: NLY), which has offered double-digit yields to its shareholders.

Nowadays Hill's investment passion is in buying Chinese micro-cap stocks, those little red racecars that can rev up one's portfolio. "It's more of a game than it is making money, at this point. I have all the money I need. It's fun, entertainment," says Hill. "I have found that for every 10 stocks that you pick, you might get one 10-bagger and a couple 3- or 4-baggers, and 3 or 4 that do nothing, and 2 that go to zero."

Strategy Tip

Negotiate with your broker. Hill makes about 25 trades on average per month mostly in penny stocks. After fleeing USAA because of high commissions, Hill was able to get TD Ameritrade to agree to a $5 per trade flat fee.

However, Hill is quick to caution investors unprepared for this sector's extreme volatility. "You can't invest in the Chinese market very long without having something just completely blow up and go to practically nothing," says Hill.

China Shoe Holdings is an example. Hill invested about $9,000 in the stock in mid-2008 starting at about $0.14 per share and after less than a year he threw in the towel after the stock had drifted to a half a penny per share. "I never knew whether the company was an out and out hoax, just badly managed, or exactly what the problem was," says Hill who typically holds about 25 Chinese stocks at any given time, spreading his risk.

When it comes to Chinese stock picks, Hill doesn't spend much time on ValueForum whose members tend to be more conservative. He uses ValueForum for finding yield and commodity stocks that account for about half of his portfolio. For Chinese micro-caps he finds the most fertile boards on InvestorVillage.com and InvestorsHub.com, Web communities where a number of Chinese investors actually post ideas.

Following the byzantine trails of message board posts, Hill will flush out stock ideas. For example, in early 2010 Hill owned a big stake in the stock of coal mining company China Energy Corp. (OTCBB: CHGY). While reading about CHGY on InvestorVillage. com's message boards, he discovered a post about another Chinese coal mining stock, Puda Coal (AMEX: PUDA). Hill did some homework and made an investment.

Strategy Tip

Use message board customization features to keep alert to new information on stocks you're tracking. When tracking stocks on InvestorVillage.com, Hill uses its MyInvestorVillage feature to monitor certain stocks and boards.

Believe it or not, one of the central tenets of Hill's strategy has nothing to do with stock picking or company analysis. It has to do with navigating the tax code. For the last few years Hill has been on a mission to convert as much of his Traditional IRA accounts into Roth IRAs as he can.

"I'm convinced that taxes are going to continue to go up with all of the spending in Washington. It is going to get much worse instead of better," says Hill, who reports that he has converted more than 80 percent of his traditional IRA accounts to Roth status.

A traditional IRA allows tax-deferred build-up of investment accounts, but upon withdrawal after age 59 1/2 the gains are taxed. Roth IRAs contain after-tax dollars to begin with and are designed to let you keep the gains you might reap from their appreciation free from federal taxes.

Converting traditional IRAs to Roths has been popular because income limitations have been lifted and the IRS is allowing people to defer the taxes they must pay as a result of the conversion process to 2011 and 2012.

Hill has applied a clever approach to the "Rothification" of his IRA accounts. Currently the law allows you to "unconvert" or recharacterize your Roth IRAs back to traditional form by as late as October 15th the year after you convert. For all intents and purposes this gives investors like Hill the benefit of 20-20 hindsight.

So in 2009 instead of converting his traditional IRA account into a single Roth IRA, he broke it up into several different accounts based on the sectors he was invested in including gold, Chinese stocks, mortgage REITs, and energy. This way, if one of these sectors went down between the time he converted and April 15, 2010, he could always recharacterize back to traditional IRA status. This would prevent the need to pay taxes on the conversion amount, which would be higher than the current value.[6]

Hill also benefits if he has a big price gain in his securities between the date of conversion of a specific IRA account into a Roth account and April 15th of the next year. This would allow Hill to convert and pay taxes on a lower (pregain) amount rather than leave it in his traditional IRA, where he would eventually need to pay taxes on his gain when he withdrew funds. This can amount to a significant tax savings.

As it turns out, 2009 was Hill's best year ever. By his calculations he had a total return of 237 percent across all of his investment portfolios, taxable and tax deferred. So his Roths went through and he had to pay a significant tax bill for 2009, but less than he would have paid if he hadn't switched.

"I think in the long run, the Roth strategy will pay huge dividends," says Hill.

Who Is Alan Hill?

Alan Hill was born in 1939, the son of an elementary school librarian and a collections manager for a city hospital in Detroit, Michigan. Hill went to Wayne State University in Detroit, majoring in business and then in about 1962 enlisted in the Navy. "I had fun in college, so I've never been a good student," says Hill.

Hill eventually got a Master's in International Business from American University in Glendale, Arizona, while still in the Navy and became an officer. He was then assigned to a ship that was stationed in the Gulf of Tonkin at the beginning of the Vietnam War.

Next, the Navy transferred him to the Defense Intelligence Agency in Washington, where Hill was expecting to put his international business education into practice, but instead was assigned to the computing department. Says Hill, "I spent most of my time getting trained by IBM to be a systems analyst in computing."

The Navy then sent Hill to the National Military Command Center at the Pentagon, but Hill disliked what he was doing. He didn't want a career in government. So after about four years he took a job in computing systems for the North Carolina Department of Education. There he eventually rose to assistant controller.

"I wanted to be in international marketing, but like a lot of people I got stuck in computing and I didn't like it," says Hill, who by then was in his early forties.

Hill saw an ad in the *Wall Street Journal* for an international education marketing manager position back in Detroit. Hill got the job, and after three years, he parlayed that experience into a position in Apple's education marketing department. So in 1985 Hill and family moved to Apple's hometown in Cupertino, California.

While at Apple, Hill was on the road for long stretches. This put a strain on his marriage, and eventually he got a divorce. In 1993 Hill moved to Indiana to work for a nonprofit in his field, The Corporation for Educational Technologies. This foundation's mission was to put computers in the homes of fourth through eighth graders and teach them computing skills. Hill eventually rose to president.

During the late 1990s Hill became an active investor in his spare time. In 1999, while researching stocks online, he stumbled across a little-followed NYSE-traded stock for one of Colombia's biggest banks, Bancolombia SA (CIB). Hill knew that most Americans only thought of Colombia as a place for coffee beans and cocaine.

"I had traveled to Colombia quite often while with Apple and was always impressed with the people I dealt with," says Hill. "The country has one of the highest standards of education in Latin America, and our subsidiary there was very well run. It seemed if they could only get the drug situation under control that the country would really blossom."

Hill figured that the best way to play a potential turnaround in Colombia was by owning a big bank that catered to the upper middle class. So Hill started buying shares of CIB in 1999 at prices near $4. Though there was talk of reform, inflation raged on in Colombia, and its economy suffered. By 2001, Bancolombia's stock had fallen to $1.40. Hill was convinced that a turnaround would happen so he bought more stock.

Says Hill, "There were starting to be stories in the press about how the new Colombian government had pledged a significant crackdown on the druglords and how the U.S. had committed millions of dollars in aid to help."

Then, in 2002, Colombia elected Álvaro Uribe Vélez as its new president. Uribe began cleaning up the nation, and the United States was pouring money in again. Bancolombia started to rebound as the nation's GDP grew and inflation came under control. Eventually Bancolombia merged with Corfinsura, the nation's largest investment bank, and Conevi, the largest mortgage bank. This strengthened the banks' position in the economy.

Hill had been active on Yahoo's message boards, but then in 2003 he defected with a bunch of other investors and became one of the first members to join the premium investor site ValueForum.com.

Hill began pounding the table on ValueForum's message boards about Bancolombia. By 2004, Hill had amassed tens of thousands of shares of Bancolombia, and in mid-2005, after the price climbed to $22, he sold enough of his CIB shares to raise $500,000.[7]

He used the money to build his pueblo-style retirement dream house in Placitas, New Mexico, where he now lives with his significant other Susan McGrath.

Their house, which is situated at an elevation of 6,300 feet, has breathtaking views all around. To the west Hill sees mesas for 40 miles. To the north from his patio he and Susan frequently observe a herd of 17 wild mustangs grazing the hills of land owned by the U.S. Bureau of Land Management. To the south there are the city lights of Albuquerque 15 miles away, and to the east Hill can see the peaks of the Sandia Mountains. Hill loves fresh bread so he built himself a special adobe-style oven where he bakes loaves a few times a week.

Hill's children are all grown up now and living in California. His daughter Lisa is a homemaker who also works as a massage therapist, and his son Thom is a former surfer who is now the CEO of Coastal Classics, a T-shirt company based in Ventura. Thom recently acquired the rights to the "Old Guys Rule" brand and is opening its first retail store in Hawaii. Hill is very proud of his children and enjoys spending time with his four grandkids.

Alan Hill is making more money now than ever. He doesn't worry about retirement income or Social Security. Hill holds the mortgage on his former house in Indiana, has several investment properties and a lakefront home on Lake Huron in Ontario, Canada. Hill also owns a 68-acre loblolly pine tree farm in Virginia that was planted 22 years ago.

Thanks to Bancolumbia and Hill's intelligent network of online investor friends, Hill has achieved a retirement nirvana that most people only dream about.

Hill's Rules of Investing

- **Go where the money and growth are.**

  Many investors try to be contrarian in their investing. Hill advises to go with the flow. That is why he has made money in sectors like energy, gold and most recently emerging markets stocks.

- **Do your homework! Read, read, and then follow up on the leads you get.**

  Hill spends more than four hours a day just reading online. He is either reading message board postings or company information and news. Sometimes he describes himself as a good listener able to tell the smart posters from the blowhards.

"Some of my friends see me, and they want to make money in the market, but they never really look at it, never read anything. They just want a tip and never follow up," says Hill. "Then they wonder why they're not successful."

- **You can't cherry pick Chinese and other risky stocks. So diversify.**

   Hill admits that "pump and dumps" and other scams are a real threat in some of the more obscure micro-cap sectors he invests in like China. He advises buying a basket of stocks. Hill's basket contains 25 or so equities. Hill tries to limit individual stocks to no more than 7 percent of his total portfolio value.

- **Minimize your mistakes.**

   Hill's favorite quote is "You only have to do a few things right in your life so long as you don't do too many things wrong." He claims that this has guided his investment philosophy. Says Hill, "If you keep looking for investment opportunities and are able to contain the inevitable mistakes that you will make along the way, every so often you are going to hit upon a HudBay Minerals, a Yamana Gold, or a China Energy, and they are going to more than equal the returns on everything else that you have made up until that time."

- **Pay attention to taxes!**

   Says Hill, "It's very, very important to get as much of your investment capital as you possibly can into a tax-free environment because if it's in a taxable account then the government is going to take a huge amount of your gains." Hill recently converted nearly all of his traditional IRAs into Roth IRAs.

Case Study: China Energy Corp. (OTCBB: CHGY)

Alan Hill's experience with one of his biggest holdings, China Energy, is a good example of how he goes about discovering undervalued micro-cap stocks.

One of the investment themes Hill has been devoted to in recent years is China. Like many others Hill believes that the ascendance of China as a dominant global economic power is inevitable. So Hill spends a lot of time researching Chinese stocks to buy.

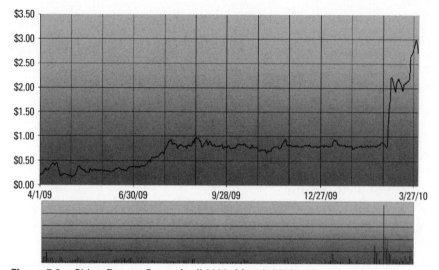

Figure 5.2 China Energy Corp., April 2009–March 2010
Source: © TickerTech.com, 2010.

Hill could easily buy an ETF or one of the Chinese big caps listed trading actively in the United States. But popular stocks like Baidu (NASDAQ: BIDU) or China Mobile (NYSE: CHL) are of little interest to Hill. Instead, he scans the boards for Chinese micro-caps and penny stocks.

About a year ago while reading through message boards posts on InvestorVillage.com, he discovered a particularly insightful poster going by the name of "Northernlights," who was an active investor in Chinese stocks.

Using the web site's private messaging tools alanthill and Northernlights started communicating about various stocks. Hill soon found out that Northernlights was actually a PhD scientist from China living in Saskatchewan and working for a large international contract research organization. Northernlights traveled to China often.

Northernlights told Hill about China Energy (see Figure 5.2), a coal mining and power company that provides heat and power to people and municipalities in Inner Mongolia. China Energy went public in 2004 in the United States via a reverse merger with a Nevada shell company.

At the time CHGY was trading at about $0.40, but shares seemed to move lower every day. Northernlights owned a lot of the stock, and he told Hill that he had spoken to management to get an update about what was going on at the company.

It turns out that the company's results were being negatively impacted by new Chinese regulations that were forcing it to halt its operations in order to install safety measures in its coal mines.

Apparently China's coal mining industry has been plagued by fires and explosions inside its mines. The majority of the China Energy's shares are owned by its chief executive WenXiang Ding and his family members. The fledgling public company had yet to hire an investor relations firm, so there was little information coming out of the company.

This partly explained the company's declining quarterly earnings that had fallen to a loss of $0.03 per share by the third quarter ending August 2009.

Worries over the global financial crisis also weighed heavily on the stock. After reading through China Energy's SEC documents and web sites and corroborating as much of Northernlight's story as he could, Hill was convinced it was a good time to get in.

Hill figured that under normal circumstances the company could earn $0.50 per share. When he first started tracking the stock in late 2008 it was selling at less than $0.40 a share. China Energy's stock wound up trading as low as $0.04 per share.

Hill ultimately accumulated 500,000 shares of China Energy at an average cost of about $0.35 "I was having a terrible year. I was trying to figure out what to do to salvage the year. It seemed like everything anybody bought seemed to go down," says Hill.

"There were probably five or six of us that were communicating and talking about this stock on InvestorVillage for six or eight months," says Hill, "One of the things that appealed to us is that management, who owned most of the stock, had not sold a single share, so we felt pretty good about the investment."

Strategy Tip

Reverse mergers are a way for companies to become publically traded entities without going through an arduous and expensive initial public offering. Many micro-caps or penny stocks start out this way. They are extremely risky and subject to manipulation. Buyer beware.

Northernlights's information was accurate. The mine reopened, and the stock began to recover and rose to around $0.70 a share, a nice return for Hill. Then China Energy released its fourth quarter 2009 earnings of 14.6 cents per share.

"Bam! After this report came out the stock went from $0.80 to $2.20 in about four days," says Hill. As of late March 2010 its stock traded for $2.70, and Hill believed its stock was still cheap based on his conservative $0.50 per share earnings estimate. That would give China Energy a trailing price earnings ratio of about five versus 16 for bigger Chinese coal stocks like Yanzhou Coal Mining (NYSE: YZC).

"One of the things that's kind of fun is that when you look at China Energy's stock price movement now, every time it goes up a penny, that's $5,000 for me. That's kind of entertaining," quips Hill on a week in late March 2010 when China Energy's share's climbed $0.60.

Hill
In His Own Words

On China's Emergence

China will morph into capitalism . . . it is well on the way to that goal today. I am amazed at some of the naysayer comments from those who have never conducted business with the Chinese, traveled there, or done any serious study of their economy. China will dominate the economies of this century.

—*March 2010, ValueForum.com*

On Change

I have always felt that the one attribute that separated successful folks from the not-so-successful folks at Apple when I worked there was how easily they adapted to change . . . because if you can't adapt to change you don't last long in the Apple environment. Along with some basic lessons in personal finance at the high school level, which nobody seems to teach, I have always believed that a course that forced students to adapt more comfortably to radically different ways of doing things under a stressful environment might equip them better to function in a world where you either will adapt or perish.

—*May 2007, ValueForum.com*

CHAPTER

Ramblin' Jack

Investor: Jack Weyland

Date of Birth: April 12, 1977

Hometown: Reno, Nevada

Personal Web Site: None

Employment: Full-time investor, former truck driver

Passions/Pursuits: Music, sports fan

Investment Strategy: Value investing, biotech stocks

Brokerage Accounts: Scottrade

Key Strategy Metric: Cash

Online Haunts: www.marketocracy.com, www.fiercebiotech.com, www.thestreet.com, www.seekingalpha.com

Best Pick: Iomai, Up 573 percent

Worst Pick: Medivation, Down 63 percent

Performance Since July 2002: Average annual return of 36 percent versus 7 percent for the S&P 500[1]

When Jack Weyland was a trucker driving thousands of highway miles each week, he often encountered dense early morning fog in central California. It's called tule fog, and it's the leading cause of weather-related casualties in California. It is the kind of fog that paralyzes most drivers forcing them to pull off the road.

But when you get paid to haul tractor-trailers full of merchandise, time spent sitting on the side of the highway is dead time. So you learn how to cope with the fog. Weyland found that music helped calm him, getting him into a zone while driving through the fog.

"You slow down. You don't use your brights, and you keep a good distance from the red lights in front of you," says Weyland, who would drive with a heightened alertness for hazards in the mist. "I would always make it to my destination."

In many ways Weyland's approach to California's fog is an appropriate metaphor for his approach to the risk that paralyzes investors pursuing profits in a volatile market. Most investors "pull over" or avoid investing in the riskier areas of the market. They play it safe, parking their money in big mutual funds or index funds that mirror the broad market.

But Jack Weyland chooses to navigate a course through one of the riskier areas of the stock market, the biotech and medical technology sectors. It's a niche where there are many more minefields and regulatory risks than there are portfolio wins. Indeed one key to Weyland's success has been his ability to mitigate the risks during his journey.

Since July 2002 Weyland has left an impressive wake on virtual money management site Marketocracy.com. In nearly eight years his Health Science Opportunities Fund (VALUE), which focuses on biotech and other health care stocks, has logged an average annual return of 36 percent per year versus about 7 percent for the S&P 500 (see Figure 6.1). About two-thirds of the stocks he picks are winners.

Over the same period of time, Vanguard's Health Care Fund (VGHCX), managed by acclaimed portfolio manager Edward Owens, had an average annual return of 5.6 percent. An investment of $10,000 in Owen's Vanguard fund would have yielded $15,202.69 from July 2002 to April 2010. An investment in Merrill Lynch's Biotech HOLDRs ETF (NYSE: BBH), an index of biotechnology stocks, would have earned slightly more, appreciating to $15,764.91.

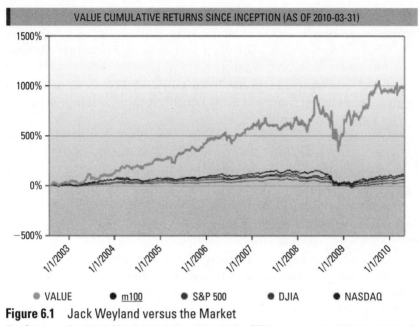

Figure 6.1   Jack Weyland versus the Market

Note: Returns are after all implied fees including 5c/share transaction fees; SEC fees; management and administration fees of 1.95 percent.

Source: Marketocracy.com; data as of March 31, 2010.

However, if you had been able to invest in Jack Weyland's Health Science Opportunities fund, which is subject to Marketocracy's $0.05 per share commission costs and a 1.95 percent fee charge, your $10,000 would be have grown to more than $109,000.

Despite his incredible performance stats, it's unlikely that Jack Weyland would have even been considered for a position as a junior analyst at a professional money management firm like Vanguard or Fidelity. Jack is a college dropout who has bounced between vocations and vacations for years. Stick-to-it-iveness is not Jack's strong suit. For 15 years Jack has been searching for his calling, and thanks to the Internet and Marketocracy, he may have found it as a stock picker.

Buying Hiccups

If you ask Jack Weyland how he has managed to be so adept at selecting great health care stocks, you won't get the kind of answer you would hear from a portfolio manager at any major investment house.

"I have developed this interface where I can filter through a lot of information now and make correct judgments when other people can't," is a typical response from Weyland. Follow up with Jack in an attempt to get more detail on that "interface" and he will talk in circles never really explaining his process.

Weyland may have some difficulty articulating his methodology for selecting stocks, but when probed about specific holdings, he has near-encyclopedic knowledge of biotech companies and the niches they operate in. Weyland's trading data explains a lot. He is a value investor who buys promising biotech stocks after they have had some bad news, often a temporary setback that the market is overreacting to. He calls them "hiccups."

Weyland spends hours reading about health care and biotechnology online. He frequents company web sites, listens to earnings calls, and will seek out peer review articles to familiarize himself with current academic opinions of drugs in the pipeline.

One web site he uses as a base for news and information on biotech companies is called FierceBiotech (www.fiercebiotech.com). This site devotes a lot of its coverage to clinical trials, potential mergers and partnerships in the industry, and things going on at the FDA. Weyland is also a big follower of The Street.com columnist Adam Feuerstein, who is renowned for his unabashed views of biotech stocks and the FDA.

"He's brilliant; I read his stuff every day," says Weyland. In fact, Weyland apparently read about one of his biggest winners, Indevus Pharmaceuticals (NASDAQ: IDEV) in Feuerstein's column.

Lexington, Massachusetts–based Indevus specializes in drugs treating urological conditions and endocrinology. One of its most promising treatments is a long-acting injectable of testosterone called Nebido. Apparently millions of men are afflicted with a condition known as hypogonadism or low testosterone. Nebido is a treatment that turbo-charges male libidos—it improves sex drive and oftentimes one's mood as well. It's a drug that is tailor-made for baby boomers and their affinity for lifestyle drugs. Can you imagine the potential of a drug you take four times a year that makes men aged 50-plus feel like they are 18 again?

Even more compelling to investors was the fact that Nebido has been in use in Europe since 2003. In fact, Indevus didn't actually invent Nebido, it merely acquired the U.S. rights to it from Bayer Schering Pharma AG, which sells it overseas. Most thought FDA approval in the United States would be a slam dunk.

However, during the final testing a single patient experienced a brief episode of coughing and shortness of breath, a side effect that was disclosed on European packaging. This prompted the FDA to send Indevus back for safety testing in the middle of 2008 shortly before most thought it would hit the market. The company announced that the setback would delay approval in the United States for two years. Indevus' stock plummeted by 75 percent to $1.65 (see Figure 6.2).

Feuerstein wrote about Indevus' setback in June 2008 just after the FDA made its announcement. Wrote Feuerstein, "The FDA stinks!"

Weyland apparently read Feuerstein's column and immediately took an interest in the stock. Weyland loves to buy beaten-down bio-tech stocks, especially when he thinks the market has overreacted to bad news.

Weyland didn't merely rely on Feuerstein's column, though; he read as much about the company as he could online, listened to earnings calls, and checked its balance sheet.

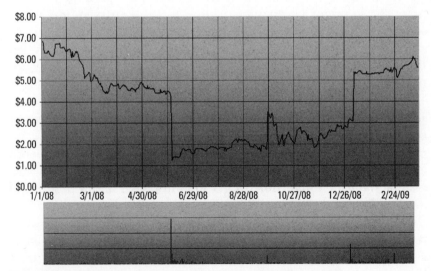

Figure 6.2   Indevus Pharmaceuticals, January 2008–March 2009

Source: © TickerTech.com, 2010.

"They had an unforeseen delay in movement of their testosterone product," says Weyland. "It's very illogical because the product is approved everywhere else except here, and the thing [coughing] that they're concerned about never occurred in the clinical trials."

Confident that Indevus's balance sheet was solid and convinced that the setback was temporary, he purchased more than 700,000 shares of Indevus for his Marketocracy account during July, August, and September of 2008. His prices ranged from $1.87 to $1.96. He also purchased the stock for his real-life brokerage account as well.

Several months later in early 2009 Endo Pharmaceuticals, apparently agreeing with Weyland's analysis, decided to acquire Indevus for $370 million or $4.50 per share, including a bonus of $3 per share if Indevus met certain milestones. Weyland made a tidy profit as he sold his shares at prices ranging from $2.87 to $5.81. He now owns Endo and is fully expecting Indevus's testosterone booster Nebido (now known as Aveed) to become a blockbuster.

Besides urology, Weyland says he focuses on finding the stocks of companies making the "best" drugs for treating Alzheimer's, diabetes, cancer, and multiple sclerosis. He also buys stocks that specialize in drug delivery and immunology.

When he does make a purchase, he is mindful of the volume in his target companies. "I like to seek entry points when sellers have dried up and signs of accumulation are starting," says Weyland who points out that it can take a decade to get through the FDA's approval process. "Hiccups," he says, are not uncommon.

In narrowing down his search for winning stocks Weyland pays special attention to the cash each of his companies has versus their burn rate. This is especially critical for smaller biotechs that raise cash via initial public offerings and spend the money on research and development. Weyland looks for a cash cushion that will give his companies enough time to get FDA approval and a product to market.

For example, one stock that Weyland bought on weakness after it suffered a delay is Pain Therapeutics (NASDAQ: PTIE). It is developing a gel form of the opiate pain remedy OxyContin called Remoxy. The key with Remoxy is that can't be abused by recreational users and addicts.

In mid-2008 its New Drug Application (NDA) was accepted by the FDA and given a Priority Review. Six months later the FDA issued a Complete Response Letter to Pain Therapeutics and its partner King Pharmaceuticals (NYSE: KG). The letter meant Remoxy would not be approved in its present form.

Pain's stock plummeted from a high of about $10 in mid-2008 to under $4 by early 2009. The sharp drop alerted Weyland to the stock, which he put on his watch list in part because it had a strong cash position. "If you did your research you would have seen that Pain is actually a very conservative company. It had more than $170 million in cash, and they were only burning cash at about $4 million a quarter. Its market cap was about $200 million," says Weyland.

Pain and King met with the FDA and then announced in July 2009 that they had a "clear path" to resubmitting Remoxy. Weyland started buying in August 2009 when shares were trading at $4.60 and took some profits in early 2010 with shares over $6. By April 2010 he still held a large stake in the stock, waiting for drug approval.

"They have an asset that isn't currently priced in, because it got delayed, and people are incorrectly perceiving that as a rejection," says Weyland.

In general Weyland likes to limit his holdings to no more than 20 stocks at any given time, so his portfolio is sometimes concentrated. Occasionally certain stocks can represent 10 percent to 20 percent of his holdings.

Weyland is mindful of the short interest in stocks on his watch list and in his portfolio. He readily admits that he has not been trained as an analyst so if he sees a buildup in short interest it makes him nervous. "Professional shorts can often be right, or they can manipulate a stock price," he says.

One book that Weyland says greatly affected his approach to stock picking is *The Psychology of Judgment and Decision Making* by

Strategy Tip

The Financial Industry Regulatory Authority (FINRA) requires brokers to report short interest or the number of shares "sold short" in a given stock. Looking at short interest relative to average volume gives investors an idea of negative sentiment in a company. Jack Weyland monitors this ratio on all his investments.

Scott Plous, PhD. The book analyzes how our inherent biases undermine our ability to weigh alternatives rationally and objectively. This clouds our decision making. The book explains and analyzes heuristics and exposes common traps decision makers face.

Heuristics is a fancy way of describing common-sense approaches to solving problems, using one's experiences as opposed to an in-depth analytical or scientific analysis. Weyland feels strongly that most of the professionals advising health care investors and bio-tech funds get lost in their spreadsheets. Weyland never completed college and has no formal training in finance, so the idea that some-one could master a "commonsense" approach is naturally appealing to him. "The biotech world is the riskiest place, and to be compet-ing with Pharma Ds, MBAs, PhDs, and MDs is not really logical," says Weyland.

He adds, "Analyst reports are well written with plenty of numbers and 'analysis' that back up their conclusions. These can appear compelling because of the overwhelming amount of data analysis; but their conclusions can be wrong. Detailed information is not a substitute for judgment, but it often is used that way."

"I develop my strategy from real-world events and perspectives. I am not here to try to pretend that I can simulate how a molecule is going to interact with receptors and whatnot. That's the folly of everybody else," says Weyland. "They all pretend that they are smart enough to comprehend how things are going to be interacting with the human body. All I care about are results, timing, and validity."

Thus for Jack Weyland one of the most important aspects of investing is breaking down potential investments and decisions into their simplest form. In some ways it's like driving through thick fog slowly, tuning out all distractions, and focusing on the red lights of the car in front of you.

Says Weyland, "I look at the potential success of a drug simply by asking, Does it solve a real problem? Do the benefits justify the risks to the patient? Is it superior to what is already on the market and is there a pent-up demand?"

Weyland's approach has produced impressive results, though like most biotech investors he isn't immune to the occasional stock disaster. One stock that hurt his portfolio in early 2010 was Medivation (NASDAQ: MDVN). The company had a very promising Alzheimer's drug called Dimebon. In the 1980s Dimebon had been used as a hay fever pill in Russia. However, more recently scientists claimed that that Dimebon also was effective in staving off mental decline in Alzheimer's patients for as long as 18 months.

After reporting impressive Phase II clinical trials held in Russia, the small San Francisco company submitted the drug for Phase III clinical trials with Pfizer footing the bill for most of the development. However, in March 2010 Medivation unexpectedly announced that the pills had worked no better than a placebo after six months.

Medivation's stock plummeted 65 percent in a single day, and Weyland promptly sold out of his shares losing as much as 63 percent of his investment. "I felt confident about Medivation because the largest pharmaceutical company in the world became involved. It would have been a huge blockbuster, but I got caught," he admits.

Weyland adds, "Usually, I'm not wrong like that. It was very bizarre situation coming after perfect Phase II trials."

Who Is Jack Weyland?

Jack Weyland, 33, was raised in Marin County outside of San Francisco. He prefers not to talk about his biological father but will only say that he was in the military. His father apparently split from his mother early in Jack's upbringing and had little to do with his life. His mother, who works in the music business, raised her only child Jack, and they remain close.

Weyland remembers that he first became interested in the market in high school. At the time he was the varsity team captain of Marin's Redwood High School basketball team. In tenth grade Weyland read *The Wall Street Journal's Guide to Understanding Money and Investing*, and it eventually inspired him to create and manage a $5,000 mutual fund for his senior class project. Weyland thought he might want to become a fund manager when he grew up. He applied to the University of Pennsylvania but was rejected, and ultimately enrolled in the University of Indiana as a business major.

However, by the time sophomore year at Indiana rolled around, Weyland decided he wasn't being challenged. "I was questioning the value of propositions of my school on a practical standpoint. From a spiritual standpoint, I recognized that I really was not developing properly in terms of managing friendships. I became someone that I'm not," says Weyland. Apparently Weyland got a little too caught up in his fraternity and social scene.

So Weyland dropped out of Indiana and decided to travel around the country in his car, visiting national parks and pondering life. He sold his 1995 Jetta and bought a cheaper used car to finance his travels, plus he used some money that he had inherited from his grandparents. That lasted for about four years but ultimately says Weyland, "It was a waste of time. I didn't yield any kind of significant results."

So in 1999 Weyland decided that a good option for him would be to enlist in the United States Air Force. "I needed some structure and serving in the military provides some significant bank to young people," says Weyland referring to the fact that he could save most of his salary.

"I chose the Air Force because of my desire for no combat. During basic training I only got to shoot a rifle for like an hour," says Weyland. Weyland tested high in his military entrance exams, so he was assigned training for a radar technician spot in their AWACs (Airborne Warning and Control System) area.

Unfortunately, Weyland ultimately failed important electronics tests that would have allowed him to advance into AWACs as a radar technician. He claims that he was then given the option by his commanding officer: be deployed to another unit or leave the Air Force with a general discharge under honorable conditions.

Weyland left the military and took a job as a baggage handler at San Francisco's International Airport. He worked mostly for regional airlines including SkyWest. "I worked the ramp at SFO. I love planes," says Weyland.

In the beginning of 2002 Weyland began taking an interest in the stock market again. At some point he saw an interview with Marketocracy CEO Ken Kam on CNBC, who explained that his web site offered aspiring money managers a virtual million-dollar mutual fund. The proposition was this: Prove that you can produce an outstanding track record and Marketocracy will let you share in the profits from the money they manage based on your picks.

So in July 2002 Weyland began managing his Health Sciences Opportunity Fund on Marketocracy.com. He used his break time at the airport as well as time outside of work to research stocks for his portfolio. At first Weyland created several Marketocracy mutual funds but began to delete the ones that weren't successful. That's how Weyland settled on health care and biotech.

About 65 percent of the trades he makes in his health and science fund are winners, and his gain/loss ratio on closed positions is 3.5 to 1.

However, Marketocracy wasn't paying Weyland's bills so in 2006 he answered an online advertisement from Schneider National, a large Wisconsin-based trucking company that was offering free training.

"I was like, that sounds pretty cool," says Weyland who eventually relocated to Reno, Nevada, after he became a regular driver for Kmart stores on the West Coast. "I found out this is actually like a perfect job for me. All I did was drive, listen to music and satellite radio, including Bloomberg news. And I had a Verizon Internet card for my laptop."

Jack Weyland became efficient about using his mandatory break times to surf the Web to do research and tend to his stock portfolio.

A typical day for Weyland might start out by picking up his load of merchandise at Kmart's distribution center in Sparks Nevada, at 2 a.m. He would then drive, often through California fog, to his first destination in Chico, California, arriving about the time the stock market opens in New York City.

While Kmart employees were unloading his tractor-trailer he would log on to the Web and check his stocks, read news, and do some research. Weyland became familiar with various "friendly" parking lots and rest stops along the West Coast that would allow him to stop every three or four hours to check the market.

After 14 hours working or 11 cumulative hours driving, Weyland, like all other truckers, would be forced to take a mandatory 10-hour Department of Transportation rest.

"When I took my DOT, I would almost always be on the Internet, trying to familiarize myself with areas like immunology, reading peer review articles, and generally doing a lot of research," says Weyland who enjoyed life as a trucker in part because Schneider used Freightliner Century–class semis. These spacious trucks had high ceilings in their cabs, were equipped with air-conditioning, beds, refrigerators, and satellite TV.

In fact, after a while Weyland gave up his apartment and lived in his truck and in cheap hotels so that he could save money to build his up real-life portfolio. Using the money he saved, plus profits from his investing, Weyland finally quit his Schneider job in the spring of 2008.

"I really hated living in the truck during the summertime," says Weyland referring to the timing of his departure and Schneider's policy of restricting truck idling time and thus air-conditioning use. Sometimes Weyland would be forced to take his mandatory DOT stopovers in Southern California where temperatures would climb to 110 degrees Fahrenheit during the day. "It becomes like an oven in the truck," he says.

Today Weyland lives modestly in an apartment in Reno, Nevada, and devotes his full attention to managing his stock portfolio.

Weyland's Rules of Investing

- **Seek out promising companies that are undervalued because of temporary setbacks or hiccups.**

  Like other successful value investors Weyland keeps an eye on stocks that have fallen abruptly. He looks for stocks of companies with temporary problems that Wall Street has overreacted to. Experienced biotech investors know that a drug's path through testing to market is rarely linear. There are inevitable setbacks. This causes volatility in stock prices, which Weyland often takes advantage of.

- **Seek entry points in stocks after sellers have dried up and signs of accumulation are beginning.**

  Though Weyland's strategy is more fundamental than technical, he does keep an eye on price and volume movements when he is ready to buy into a position. He mostly uses weekly candlestick charts, which display high, low, open, and close for a stock, and help investors determine if the stock is in an uptrend or downtrend. Candlestick charts can be found on web sites such as StockCharts.com, Google Finance, and Yahoo Finance.

- **Look for companies that serve an unmet medical or health care need.**

  Weyland doesn't get too wrapped up in spreadsheet modeling when making decisions to buy stocks. He has no formal training in stock analysis. He likes to keep it simple when he makes decisions on stocks and uses his own experiences as a guide. He looks for health care companies where the benefits of their products are clear and obvious. His investment in Iomai Corp. (see case study on page 98) is an example because needle-free flu and other vaccines have the potential of greatly improving vaccine acceptance and penetration globally.

- **Avoid companies with high short interest.**

    Hedge funds and short sellers love to trade biotech stocks because they are volatile and often have low floats. Weyland never wants to get into a situation where he is caught in a stock where hedge funds are trying to manipulate shares or betting heavily against a company's prospects. He therefore keeps an eye on short interest. If it's too high relative to average share volume, he stays away.

- **If the market appears to be overbought, hedge your portfolio.**

    Like many other investors, Jack Weyland's portfolio fell sharply in 2008. He currently uses inverse ETFs to hedge his portfolio when sentiment indicators and other valuations show that the market is overvalued.

- **Diversify but don't overdo it.**

    Jack Weyland runs a concentrated portfolio ranging from 10 to 20 stocks. Like others profiled in this book he doesn't feel that most managers can effectively manage a large portfolio of stocks. He also believes that too much diversification merely leads to performance that matches broad indexes. If Weyland is confident a stock is deeply undervalued, he will often commit up to 15 percent of his portfolio to that stock. This has been the case in several of his best performers including Elan (NYSE: ELN), Indevus, and Iomai. This strategy backfired on him in his investment in Medivation, which fell about 65 percent in one day after reporting bad news.

- **Try to invest without emotion or bias no matter how promising or likeable a company or its treatments are.**

    One of the cardinal rules of investing is maintaining discipline. It's easy to fall in love with a company that is developing some great remedy, like Medivation's Alzheimer's treatment Dimebon, but this will cloud your decision making when it comes to the capital you have at risk in your stock portfolio.

- **Avoid the sunk cost effect. Cut your losses and move on.**

    Many investors hold on to their losses in hopes that they will recover. Most professional investors agree that this is a bad strategy. Not all of Jack Weyland's picks have been winners, but as a rule he cuts his losses when necessary. Often times he has invested a significant amount of time in his thesis for buying a stock, however if better opportunities exist in the market, he moves on to the next investment.

Case Study: Iomai[2]

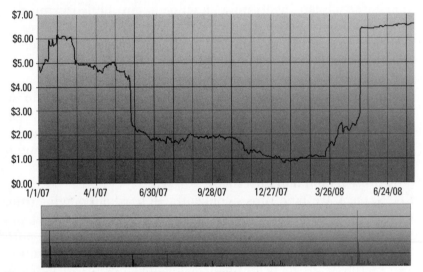
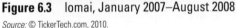

Figure 6.3   Iomai, January 2007–August 2008

Source: © TickerTech.com, 2010.

One part of the biotech world that Weyland likes to invest in is drug delivery. Gaithersburg, Maryland–based Iomai Corporation caught Weyland's attention in 2007 after a test for a flu vaccine it was delivering via skin patch ran into problems during Phase I trials.

The company had raised about $32 million via an IPO in February 2006 underwritten by UBS Investment Bank and SG Cowen at $7 per share.[3] But after the bad news came out about its patch vaccine for influenza in May 2007 institutional investors ran for the exits. Iomai's shares fell in price to under $1.

"It was a pretty big mistake to make in Phase I," says Weyland referring to the fact that this later stage of testing requires remedies to be nearly ready for market.

But Iomai fit Weyland's criteria for promising biotech companies experiencing temporary hiccups.

Weyland liked that the benefits of Iomai's remedies were relatively simple and obvious. A needle-free vaccine patch would help boost vaccination rates because it is more convenient and easier to supply and administer.

Says Weyland, "People would be surprised to learn that the skin is the largest organ or that an immune response can be initiated with a scratch and bacteria. I was amazed by this potential opportunity."

Iomai's revenue potential was significant. The market for needle-free flu patches is estimated to be in excess of $1 billion, and other indications in its pipeline, like its pandemic influenza patch and its traveler's diarrhea patch, also had $1 billion-plus market potential.[4]

Iomai had a relatively strong balance sheet. By mid-2007 Iomai still had plenty of IPO cash left; some $26 million[5] was reported as of June 30, 2007. Net losses were running about $7 million per quarter.

Says Weyland, "I was trying to set up a position where if I'm right, there's going to be a significant reward, and if I'm wrong, there's just going to be less of a reward." So Iomai went on Weyland's watch list and Weyland continued to do his research.

Weyland dug deeper into the problems that Iomai faced during its initial flu patch testing in 2007. He found that Iomai had admitted that its problem was that it had used a traditional split-virus vaccine antigen (a smaller amount) but that it was less effective than the inject-able version of the vaccine. So after reading more on the company and listening to management presentations, he became confident that they could fix this shortcoming with a stronger dose.

Weyland felt that Wall Street was completely ignoring the successes that Iomai was having with its other patches, including its traveler's diarrhea patch. There was still reasonable hope of success, but institutions were still shunning Iomai.

By watching Iomai's share volume depicted by candlestick charts, Weyland saw that the sellers had disappeared. In February 2008 as financial markets were reeling, Weyland decided the time was right. Iomai's distressed shares had fallen below $1.

Weyland made his move and within two weeks, he had accumulated nearly 400,000 shares of Iomai for his virtual Marketocracy fund at prices ranging from $0.92 to $1.14. He simultaneously bought a significant amount of the stock in his real-life brokerage account.

As it turns out, Iomai's hiccup in 2007 was just that. Iomai's needle-free patch for traveler's diarrhea sailed through its Phase II field study. It cut the risk of moderate-to-severe travelers' diarrhea by 75 percent versus a placebo patch. The company's pandemic flu vaccine patch also had positive results and support from the U.S.

Department of Health and Human Services, which awarded it a five-year cost-plus reimbursement contract.

Weyland wasn't the only one to take notice. Soon after Weyland established his position, Merck (NYSE: MRK), a pharmaceutical giant with a huge stake in the vaccine business, announced it would be working with Iomai to test its patches.[6]

By April 2008 shares of Iomai were trading at $1.76, and Weyland already had a 90 percent profit on many of his shares. Weyland held on. About a month later Austrian vaccine maker Intercell, AG (Vienna Stock Exchange: ICLL) announced that it would acquire Iomai for $6.60 per share.[7] Weyland sold out of his entire position by mid-May at a price of $6.27.

Weyland
In His Own Words

On Health Care versus Other Sectors

I became interested in health care investing 10 years ago because of the long-term demographics: aging population and increasing longevity trends but mostly because of the potential for price inefficiencies. It can take years for a promising drug to go through the FDA approval process, and rarely does that process go without hiccups. During that extended time generally problems, uncertainties, risks, fears, etc. arise and because the science behind these drugs and the disease can be complex, investors over-react and sell off.

—*2009, Marketocracy.com*

On His Approach to Investing

My goal is to not only to be right, but to be right at the right time. My strategy is to find value in assets that others throw away and to find entry points where others sold out.

—*April 2010*

CHAPTER 7

The Oracle of Manitoba

Investor: Randy McDuff

Date of Birth: January 4, 1965

Hometown: Winnipeg, Manitoba

Personal Web Site: None

Employment: Former stockbroker, currently investing full-time

Passions/Pursuits: Comic book collecting, cycling, and his three dogs

Investment Strategy: Value with a global macro twist, "Warren Buffett meets John Templeton"

Brokerage Account: Not available

Key Strategy Metric: Enterprise value/Ebitda

Online Haunts: www.marketocracy.com, www.cia.gov, www.valueinvestorclub.com

Best Pick: MasterCard, Up 606 percent

Worst Pick: Kindred Healthcare, Down 75 percent

Performance Since July 2000: Average annual return +19 percent versus −0.70 percent for the S&P 500[1]

There are few more unlikely incubators for outstanding investors than The Pas, Manitoba. Perched on the shore of the Saskatchewan River, this former trapper Mecca is sometimes called The Gateway to the North. It's a place where Hudson Bay winds can chill the air to minus 40 degrees in January and folks are accustomed to waiting eight months for winter to give way to the flowers of springtime. It's also the hometown of Randolph McDuff, an individual investor who, at age 45, has a better performance record than the vast majority of professionals who are paid millions to manage pensions, 401(k)s, mutual funds, and hedge funds.

Like most others in this book, McDuff has no fancy MBA, is not a CFA or CPA, and was not trained as a financial analyst. It may be that the education he received living in remote The Pas as a boy helped McDuff avoid the distractions that eventually become ingrained in most of us by the time we are teenagers. With only three channels on the television and no video games or bustling malls to lure him, McDuff spent the hours of his youth in the town library reading the financial papers that were delivered once a week. You could say that living in northern Manitoba helped McDuff develop those two rare but critical successful investor attributes: patience and discipline. In The Pas, Manitoba, patience and discipline are a way of life.

McDuff is one of the best stock pickers the world has never heard of. Since July 2000 the total return on his virtual portfolio (RMG1), tracked by online stock picking community Marketocracy. com, has gained 19 percent per year on average (see Figure 7.1). That compares to a –0.7 percent return for the S&P 500 during the same time period. It's a better performance record than nearly all professional stock mutual fund managers. A similarly timed investment in Warren Buffett's Berkshire Hathaway would have produced only 9 percent per year in gains. Over the last nine years the $1 million McDuff started with in his virtual portfolio has grown to $5.4 million after accounting for commissions of $0.05 a share and a 1.95 percent management fee.

Warren Buffett Meets Sir John Templeton

Like the Oracle of Omaha Warren Buffett, McDuff is a value investor. However, McDuff applies his craft with a global-macro twist.

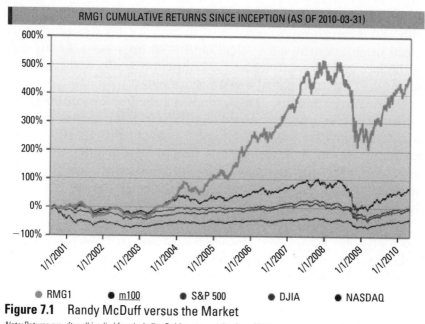

RMG1 CUMULATIVE RETURNS SINCE INCEPTION (AS OF 2010-03-31)

● RMG1   ● m100   ● S&P 500   ● DJIA   ● NASDAQ

Figure 7.1   Randy McDuff versus the Market

Note: Returns are after all implied fees including 5c/share transaction fees; SEC fees; management and administration fees of 1.95 percent.

Source: Marketocracy.com; data as of March 31, 2010.

That means that McDuff first settles on a big global trend or theme and then drills down into what he thinks is the best investment according to his thesis.

Here's how it works: If McDuff is bullish on a "top down" trend like the *expanding middle class in emerging markets,* he would then further narrow his focus to a specific industry theme such as global infrastructure or global transport. In fact, McDuff set on the theme of global transportation in 2006. Using the Internet as his library, McDuff spent hours researching publicly traded stocks related to transportation in emerging economies. He came up with several that met his valuation criteria and invested in them. Some of the stocks he bought (and still owns as of early 2010) include Mexico's Grupo Aeroportuario del Sureste (NYSE: ASR), which operates nine airports in southeast Mexico and Beijing's Capital International Airport, which is now the fourth-busiest airport in the world. He also invested in China's Guangshen Railway (NYSE: GSH), which is the only publicly traded passenger and freight railway in China with stock listed overseas.

Most of the companies in McDuff's portfolio are multinationals with extensive overseas operations. Because of his strong international orientation in stock selection, his strategy is similar to that of the late great John Templeton. Templeton is widely regarded as one of the fathers of global investing.

Like Warren Buffett, Templeton was a died-in-the-wool contrarian investor (meaning he sought to profit by going against conventional wisdom). He was also known for saying that the four most dangerous words in investing are "this time it's different." John Templeton's flagship Templeton Growth Fund, which was launched in 1954, had an impressive 14.5 percent average annual return by the time the group was sold to Franklin Resources in 1992.

You can think of Randy McDuff's investment strategy as being two parts John Templeton combined with one part Warren Buffett. So far Randy's mix of these two legendary investment styles has produced a decade-long performance record that puts him squarely on the road toward investment guru status.

Who Is Randy McDuff?

Born in January 1965 in The Pas, Manitoba, McDuff is the son of a pulp and paper mill machinist. He graduated from the University of Manitoba in 1986 with a bachelor's degree in commerce. Given his strong interest in stocks, McDuff's first job out of university was as a broker trainee at a small Winnipeg firm. A few years later, in May 1990, McDuff accepted a job at the Winnipeg branch of Nesbitt Thomson Deacon. The firm eventually became BMO Nesbitt Burns, after Bank of Montreal acquired it in 1994.

By all accounts, McDuff was one of Nesbitt's most successful brokers. In less than 10 years he had amassed more than 1,000 clients with $50 million in assets under management. In fact, during the mid-1990s, McDuff was so successful that his team, including his wife Bridget and several sales assistants, was known inside the firm as The McDuff Group. From 1994 through 1997 McDuff's clients enjoyed average annual returns of approximately 23 percent versus 19 percent for the S&P 500 over the same time period.[2] According to those who worked with him, McDuff was always innovative in his approach to investment selection, looking for values among convertible securities and high-yielding income trusts. In Canada so-called income trusts are prevalent, especially those associated with oil and gas. These trusts trade publically on stock exchanges and pay out virtually all their earnings to unit holders before paying taxes. At one point McDuff had as much as 70 percent of his client's money in income trusts.

However, in the late 1990s after Nesbitt came under the control of Bank of Montreal, the firm's compliance department tightened its grip on the Winnipeg branch. It began to worry about its resident investment maverick Randy McDuff. The bank was emphasizing packaged products and mutual funds, and McDuff was buying exotic things like trusts and convertibles. BMO Nesbit Burns's compliance department determined that The McDuff Group didn't fit the mold. It needed to be reined in.

So Randy McDuff and his team began to be monitored by the firm's compliance department. Ultimately McDuff was reprimanded for such brokerage business sins as investment suitability, the use of leverage in client accounts, and his level of commissions. He also got into trouble because one of his "snow-bird" clients lived in the United States for greater than six months inadvertently putting McDuff in violation of licensing regulations.

Of course, McDuff's clients didn't complain while he was making them high returns, but in 1998 Canada's booming oil and gas trust market crashed when oil prices dropped as low as $12 per barrel, from as high as $25 in 1996.[3] McDuff's clients got caught in the spiral and suffered big losses. McDuff apparently became distraught and frustrated when his firm's compliance department pressured him to sell his clients' trust shares despite his confidence that they would eventually recover. (Indeed by 2000 oil prices were up, and the income trust market recovered.)

Feeling personally responsible for his clients' losses McDuff sunk into a deep depression and eventually was given a medical leave of absence from the firm. At about the same time the dot-com bubble burst and stocks plummeted in Canada and in the United States. With their star broker McDuff absent during this critical time, the complaints flooded into Nesbitt Burns. McDuff's broker license was suspended, his McDuff Group was dismantled, and his client accounts were divvyed up among other Nesbitt brokers. It was an ugly end to a promising career.

McDuff won't talk about the specifics of the final days of his career as a broker at Nesbitt, only to say that he left because he was fed up and stressed out. He has few kind words for the stock brokerage business he once excelled in.

"At most firms you don't even have the time to do the job you are being asked to do," gripes McDuff. "The industry rewards stock analysts for homogeneous work and penalizes those that take unique, insightful views of companies. You are basically told who to cover and who the peer group should be."

By age 37, Randy McDuff had saved enough as a successful stockbroker to live comfortably with his wife Bridget, provided they were astute in their investment choices. The McDuffs also owned a Winnipeg car wash that provided the couple with cash flow.

It was then that McDuff turned to online stock picking community Marketocracy.com to reinvent himself. McDuff was an early volunteer among the 70,000 online investors that eventually signed up for Marketocracy.com. He set up two virtual million-dollar mutual fund portfolios on the web site. One, called RMG1, focuses on global big cap stocks and the other, called RMG2, on smaller cap companies. McDuff claims that the trades he makes in his Marketocracy funds are nearly identical to the ones he makes in real life.

So far the small amount of income McDuff derives from Marketocracy's asset management business hasn't changed his lifestyle. He continues to live in a modest home in a middle-class neighborhood on the north side of Winnipeg with his wife and three dogs Rocco, Johnny, and Maximus. And despite losses on his portfolio holdings in 2008, he continues his "retirement." Says McDuff, "I am not jet rich. But we live comfortably. In Winnipeg our quality of life is awfully good."

When McDuff is not online researching stocks or taking his dogs for walks in a nearby park, he's typically out running. Says McDuff, "For some reason, perhaps the endorphin rush that coincides with a good jog, I get to do a lot of critical thinking about investments and the economy while I exercise. Consequently, some of my best investment selections have been worked out during a healthy 10K to 15K workout."

McDuff is also an avid comic book collector. However, true to his value investor bias, he selects comics he thinks are undervalued with the hope that eventually they will become television shows, or turned into movies, causing their value to appreciate. "Comic book collecting for me is the identification of authors and comic books that, at some point down the road, will have some kind of catalyst," says McDuff.

Some of the comic books McDuff has collected include *Iron Man*, which he first began buying as a teen, and *Silver Surfer*, which first appeared in Marvel's Fantastic Four comic in 1966. He also owns early editions of D.C. comic's *Kamandi: The Last Boy on Earth*, which ran from 1972 through 1978.

"I have high hopes that *Kamandi* could be a movie because the premise is quite interesting. It's the story of a young boy who emerges from a nuclear fallout shelter. To some extent it is a take-off on *Planet of the Apes* because all of the animals are intelligent," says McDuff.

One late 1970s series that McDuff has been collecting is called *John Carter Warlord of Mars*. The Marvel comic character is based on a book series written by Edgar Rice Burroughs, the creator of *Tarzan*. It already shows signs of a catalyst, and prices for the comic book have risen in value. According to movie database web site, IMDB, *John Carter of Mars*, will be made into a movie by Disney and has recently gone into preproduction and is scheduled for release in 2012.

McDuff's Rules of Investing

- **Find stocks that are being ignored by Wall Street.**

    Like other contrarian investors, McDuff subscribes to the idea that Wall Street analysts and investors are a bit like sheep. They tend to move in herds but often in the wrong direction at the wrong time. Thus when high tech stocks were sizzling during late 1990s and amateur day traders were buying stocks like Amazon.com (NASDAQ: AMZN) and TheGlobe.com (NASDAQ: TGLO), McDuff and other contrarians shunned such volatile hot stocks. For value investors such popular stocks are overexposed and overvalued.

    However, according to McDuff, it's a mistake to believe that the only neglected stocks out there are those of smaller companies. First, Wall Street analysts have always focused most of their research on companies that have a regular need for capital. In other words, they have historically focused on the firms that also tend to be good investment banking clients. Thus many good companies that grow "organically" with internal cash flow and thus have no need for investment bankers get ignored by Wall Street.

    A few years ago, this cozy relationship between "research" and "banking" led to scandals that rocked the brokerage business. The result was a settlement that changed the economics of research coverage, and many big firms closed their stock research departments.

Today there are simply fewer professional research analysts left to analyze stocks, both small and big. So it's not just smaller capitalization stocks that are being neglected; many giant companies lack research coverage today.

One glaring example that McDuff likes to point out is Nestlé SA (pink: NSRGY), the Swiss maker of everything from instant coffee to Purina pet food, Perrier water and Häagen-Dazs ice cream. Nestlé has more than $100 billion in worldwide sales, 456 factories, and 283,000 employees. Its brands are household names around the globe, and it has stock trading both in Switzerland and in the United States over-the-counter on the pink sheets. Yet as of late 2009 only two professional stock analysts were listed as having earnings estimates for Nestlé according to Yahoo Finance. That compares to 12 analysts listed for competitor Pepsico and 15 for much smaller companies such as Kraft Foods. Believe it or not, giant Nestlé suffers from neglect. McDuff owns Nestlé in his Marketocracy portfolio.

- **Seek out companies with strong business models, preferably monopolies, duopolies, or oligopolies.**

  One of McDuff's best investments over his nine years of being tracked by Marketocracy.com is credit card payment processor MasterCard Worldwide (NYSE: MA). McDuff bought the stock soon after it went public in May 2006 at a price of $54. The stock has risen as high as $308 and fallen as low as $113 in March 2008. It remains one of McDuff's largest holdings.

  Says McDuff,"MasterCard is my preferred play for growth in global commerce. The company has more than 750 million accounts globally, and half of its total revenues come from outside the United States. The company is one of the two major global credit card processors. I consider MasterCard to have duopoly profit margins." A look at MasterCard's profitability ratios reveal operating margins of more than 40 percent versus 6 percent for American Express and 10 percent for credit card bank CapitalOne Financial. In addition, MasterCard (and Visa) carry less direct credit card default risk because it's their bank partners (like CapitalOne and

JPMorgan Chase) and owners of securitized pools of credit card receivables that are at risk.

McDuff adds that the economies of scale enjoyed by the Visa-MasterCard duopoly make it virtually impossible for competitors to compete on price. Indeed, the biggest potential threat to their dominance over the last few years has been eBay's online payment system, PayPal, which charges merchants lower fees. However, PayPal's growth has actually added to the coffers of MasterCard and Visa. PayPal's parent eBay clearly states in its annual report that "If PayPal were unable to accept credit cards, its business would be seriously damaged."

"We are moving toward a cashless society, and we are becoming globally mobile, and we need access to currency. Besides credit and debit, the next big market that I think MasterCard and Visa can dominate is the money transfer business," says McDuff. "There is no reason why I shouldn't be able to go into a convenience store or a Wal-Mart, punch in my PIN number and send money instantly to a relative in Asia."

- **Focus on enterprise value/EBITDA rather than price/earnings ratios.**

Most investors, including value investors, like to talk about P/Es or price-earnings multiples. P/Es are widely quoted in the media, but for the most part they fail to give an investor a true picture of a company's valuation because debt is excluded. Enterprise value is defined as a company's equity market capitalization plus its debt and preferred stock outstanding minus cash. Thus enterprise value gives a better indication of what it would cost to take over a company. McDuff's preferred measure of comparative value is EV/EBITDA, where EBITDA is defined as earnings before interest, taxes, depreciation, and amortization.

EBITDA is a good measure of a company's profitability because it excludes noncash expenses like depreciation and amortization. EBITDA is not cash flow or free cash flow, and many like Warren Buffett have criticized the measure because it doesn't account for real cash expenses like working capital, capital expenditures, and repayment of principal.

EBITDA, however, is widely published and quoted, which makes it easy for McDuff and others to use it as a point of comparison. As a general rule, McDuff says he likes stocks with a forward (meaning next year's) EV/EBITDA of 10 or less, but will relax the rule a bit as long as the company is a market leader and is selling at a discount to industry competitors.

- **Beware of false confidences like "Invest in What You Know."**

Randy McDuff likes to say familiarity breeds mediocrity. Ever since Peter Lynch's spectacular run at the helm of Fidelity's Magellan fund from 1977 until 1990 (Lynch's average annual return was 29 percent) and his best-seller, *One Up on Wall Street,* many investors have subscribed to his "buy what you know" philosophy. It's the idea that local knowledge should guide your stock selection. So if your kids are raving about their new Xbox videogame console, it makes sense to buy the shares of its maker, Microsoft.

While McDuff generally agrees that buying "what you know" is better than buying what you *don't* know, he argues that it can make investors lazy, thinking that good investments will always be found "at your doorstep."

"False confidence is no substitute for fundamental investment research and thorough peer analysis," says McDuff. One example McDuff cites is U.S. investors' blind devotion to big U.S.-based pharmaceutical companies such as Merck (NYSE: MRK) and Pfizer (NYSE: PFE).

Says McDuff, "Long-term investors piled in a generation ago. The lure was pie charts full of favorable demographic data on drug use. After all, these companies produce a pill for every real (or imagined) need. And as we age, don't we all consume more drugs? The business model has been touted as being recession proof."

However, over the last decade both Merck and Pfizer have lost more than 50 percent in value compared to a loss of only 4 percent for the Dow Jones Industrial Average and a loss of 20 percent for the S&P 500.

McDuff points out that this "false confidence" is especially prevalent among U.S.-based investors who tend to have a myopic view of the investment landscape. Currently one of McDuff's bigger holdings is France's Sanofi-Aventis (NYSE: SNY), the world's third-largest pharmaceutical company with $40 billion in revenues. About 70 percent of its revenues come from outside the United States, so it also gets a

Strategy Tip

Despite McDuff's affinity for online investing, he still uses a full-service broker. As a global investor, McDuff often has an easier time trading American Depositary Receipts (ADRs) and shares of non-U.S. companies with his full-service broker. Says McDuff, "I can point to numerous examples when using a full-service broker saved me time and money."

boost from foreign currencies that are appreciating against the dollar.

Sanofi is the world's leading producer of vaccines, with 21 percent of the market. It is also a leader in the diabetes market with another McDuff favorite, Denmark's Novo Nordisk (NYSE: NVO). According to McDuff, Novo and Sanofi also fit his rule that companies be oligopolistic, since they compete with just a few other companies at the top of the diabetes treatment market. Sanofi is listed on Yahoo Finance with only 2 analyst estimates for its earnings versus 15 for Pfizer.

Case Study: Companhia Brasileira de Distribuicao (NYSE: CBD)

As a global investor McDuff looks for growth companies at value prices no matter where they are located around the world. In 2009, after suffering losses in his Marketocracy portfolio but still holding fast to most of his stocks, he set out looking for bargains among the fallen stocks.

Unlike many investors who spend hours online looking for ideas on popular web sites such as Yahoo or AOL, Randy scours various government, academic, and company web sites for ideas. One of the web sites he uses for research is the Central Intelligence Agency's World Factbook, found at www.cia.gov.

"The site gives you a wonderful macroeconomic overview of the planet," says McDuff. Using this data he noticed that the global economic scene was not nearly as dire in 2008 as you would have believed watching CNBC or reading media reports.

In fact, the data on cia.gov revealed to McDuff that overall the world-wide gross domestic product (GDP) actually advanced 3.8 percent in 2008, though down from 5.2 percent. China's estimated real GDP growth was an impressive 9 percent, despite a drop from 13 percent in 2007, and the plummeting of its stock market.

Analyzing the CIA web site data, McDuff began to take a keen interest in Brazil, which had an estimated real GDP growth rate of 5.1 percent in 2008, only down slightly from 2007, when it was 5.7 percent.

"In 2008 Brazilian GDP leapfrogged my home country of Canada to become the tenth-largest economy in the world. I think by the end of 2010 it will overtake Russia, which is now number seven," says McDuff.

He goes on: "Brazil is pro-business, and it features low corporate taxes and a better national balance sheet than most big economies. When I look at its economy and prospects, I see a nation featuring China's growth potential, but without China's problematic lack of strategic natural resources. Also, only 2 percent of Brazilian GDP comes from the United States." For McDuff this lack of dependence on the United States is a big plus, considering the financial pressures and economic obstacles likely facing Americans in the coming years.

McDuff then drilled even deeper trying to determine whether Brazilian stocks were still a bargain given the attention some of its big companies like Petroleo Brasileiro (Petrobras, NYSE: PBR) have received. McDuff noted that in 2008 Brazil's $1.67 trillion GDP was 2.4 percent of global GDP. This is similar to Canada's GDP that represented 2.2 percent of global GDP. However, Canada, which has suffered an anemic real GDP growth rate, had a publically traded stock market value of $2.2 trillion or 3.3 percent of all the stock markets around the world.

Brazil's fast-growing stock market valuation amounted to just 2 percent of the world's stock market capitalization. Hence Brazil's economy, while 7 percent larger than Canada's and growing much faster, had a stock market valuation at the end of 2008 that is only

Strategy Tip

The best investment ideas don't necessarily come from popular investment web sites like Yahoo Finance or AOL. McDuff uses government sites like www.CIA.gov, company web sites, and academic journal web sites like Social Science Research Network www.ssrn.com.

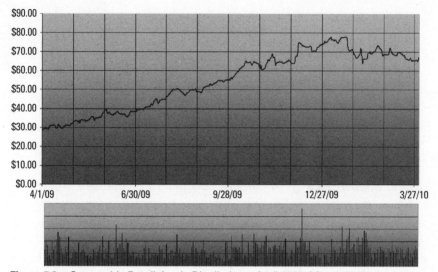

Figure 7.2   Companhia Brasileira de Distribuicao, April 2009–March 2010

Source: © TickerTech.com, 2010.

62 percent as high as Canada's. These stats gave McDuff confidence that buying selected Brazilian equities was a sound bet from a macroeconomic perspective.

McDuff also discovered that only 10 of approximately 440 publically traded companies on Brazil's stock exchange account for more than half of its market capitalization. For a value investor that means there are lots of potentially undervalued firms to uncover in Brazil.

McDuff's first major buy among Brazilian stocks was Companhia Brasiliera de Distribuicao (see Figure 7.2), its largest grocery and general goods retailer. Its shares trade on the NYSE as an ADR under the symbol CBD. Think of CBD as a Brazilian version of Wal-Mart. The $10 billion (revenues) company has nearly 600 stores in 14 Brazilian states and has a 13 percent share of the Brazilian food market.

CBD's stores operate under banners including Pao de Acucar, an upscale neighborhood grocery chain; CompreBem, a supermarket chain for families on a lower budget; and Extra, a hypermarket-grocery and general merchandise chain. It also owns a retail chain called Extra Eletro that sells furniture, house wares, flat screen televisions, and other electronics. The company's founder and chairman is Brazilian billionaire Abilio dos Santos Diniz.[4]

Strategy Tip

Before Randy McDuff pulls the trigger on a stock he has been eyeing, he writes an 1,000-plus word analysis explaining his thesis. This helps him to confirm his facts and focus his reasoning. He posts some of his reports on Marketocracy.com and has also put others on ValueInvestorsClub.com, an exclusive value investor web site (see Chapter 11).

McDuff is betting that CBD will thrive as Brazilian incomes rise. McDuff reports that the company has healthier margins than U.S. and Canadian companies, and is growing more rapidly. Its balance sheet is strong, and it is one of the three top food retailers in Brazil. CBD, France's Carrefour, and Wal-Mart account for 39 percent of the entire market. As for pricing, McDuff was able to purchase CBD at a forward enterprise value to Ebitda ratio of about 10 during mid-2009 as the shares were recovering from Brazil's market decline in 2008.

McDuff
In His Own Words
On Utilities and Recession-Resistant Stocks

Years ago, it used to be that a utility was considered to be a dry, dull, bread-and-butter investment. You know, people could count on them for dividends. People could basically sleep at night owning them. But what has happened is there has been a great pressure put upon the managements of many of these companies to enhance or improve their earnings. And the only way to do so has been to add elements of risk to their business plans. The pure recession-resistant industries have deliberately and strategically made business decisions that increase risk.

—July 2009

Post–2008 Crash Investing

I believe that volatility going forward will also increase, as it should. The corollary to all of this is that if volatility is going to increase and investments from a business perspective on the whole are now riskier than before, investors, therefore, should expect or anticipate higher returns from their portfolios in order to compensate.

Years ago, if you could get 6 or 7 percent from a blue-chip portfolio that would be satisfactory. Now, I think we're going to have to look to earn more.

—July 2009

On Retirement Investing

Here's how I planned my retirement: I built a portfolio of securities that paid modest dividends. I didn't put more than 2 percent of my portfolio in any one security. I didn't put more than 10 percent of my account in any one industry. The companies selected had to pay dividends that were less than 35 percent of their after tax income to qualify. I kept buying these stocks until the dividend income earned from that account matched my pretax employment income.

Then, I could afford to retire. I would never want to be in a position where I would have to sell stocks in a bear market. I could go on a one-year holiday and not have to watch my portfolio. With enough stocks and periodic dividend increases that exceed inflation (over time) I probably won't ever run out of income.

So here's "my" magic number. If you need to match $120,000 of pretax employment income and you can only find a portfolio that will pay you 2 percent dividends, then you'll need $6 million. If you can build a portfolio that pays you closer to 3 percent then you'll need $4 million. In short, bank on a 2 percent to a 3 percent dividend yield, and figure out what you'll need to invest to match that income. Then, you can retire in style!

—May 2006, Marketocracy.com

On New Money versus Old Money

There are two types of people in the investment world: Those who equate personal success by the size of their account or with whom they are affiliated with. This is the problem with "new money." They flaunt it.

There are those who don't talk specifically about their financial wealth. It's a given that they have it, so why would they announce it? This is the attribute noted with "old money." I'm new money, but I want to not be tarred with the same brush of new money.

—October 2009

Mexican Gold

Investor: Andrew Swann

Date of Birth: April 26, 1954

Hometown: San Miguel de Allende, Mexico

Personal Web Site: None

Employment: Full-time investor

Passions/Pursuits: Fishing, tennis, and history

Investment Strategy: Junior gold stocks, oil, gas, hard assets

Brokerage Accounts: E*Trade

Key Metric: Cash flow

Online Haunts: www.valueforum.com, www.SmartInvestment.ca

Best Pick: Desert Sun Mining, Up more than 1,000 percent

Worst Pick: Oilexco Inc., Down 92 percent

Performance Since September 2004: Cumulative return of 237 percent versus 11 percent for the S&P 500[1]

Never underestimate the importance of good timing. Even the most accomplished investors will admit to this truism. The subject of this chapter, Andrew Swann, is an outstanding investor because his specialty has been gold and other commodity stocks like oil. In fact, gold and energy stocks have represented more than half of his investment portfolio for the last decade. During that time the price of one ounce of gold has soared from $300 to more than $1,100. Oil has also skyrocketed, rising from under $30 per barrel to a high of $147 in 2008.

Swann started investing in gold in 1996, but he became convinced that he should sell most of his other investments and become more fully invested in gold by January 2003. Since then he says his stock portfolio has risen nearly 600 percent in value. An investment in the SPDR S&P 500 ETF (NYSE: SPY) over the same period would have yielded a total return of 39 percent. I have not verified this by checking his brokerage statements, but I have good reason to believe he is an outstanding investor. ValueForum.com has tracked Swann's performance in its stock-picking contests since late 2004 (see Figure 8.1). If you had invested $10,000 in Swann's quarterly entries you would have accumulated $33,700 as of March 31, 2010 versus $11,100 for a similar investment in the S&P 500.

However, what those impressive numbers don't show is the life-style successes that Swann has achieved at a relatively young age thanks to his smart and opportunistic approach to investing.

Most professional investors obsess over measuring relative performance compared to indexes like the S&P 500 or the Dow Jones Industrial Average. The media reinforce the importance of this every day. In fact, the verifiable track record of every investor profiled in this book is measured against the S&P 500.

We are all very impressed when someone like Bill Miller and his Legg Mason Value Trust outperforms the S&P 500 for 15 years in a row. I don't know how many times I have heard money managers or their PR people boast to me about beating the S&P the year prior by 100 basis points (1 percentage point) and feeling very proud of themselves despite the fact that the S&P may have only advanced 6 percent.

But this is not what people really care about or what I think is important. What is important is having the financial resources to

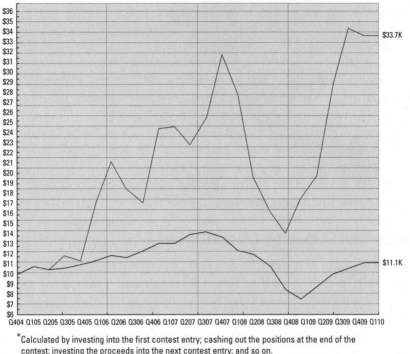

$10K into swannmex's entries vs. invested into the S&P 500*

*Calculated by investing into the first contest entry; cashing out the positions at the end of the contest; investing the proceeds into the next contest entry; and so on.

Figure 8.1   Andrew Swann versus the S&P 500

Source: © TickerTech.com; data as of March 31, 2010, swannmex = Andrew Swann's screen name on ValueForum.com.

achieve one's goals: Living the life you want to live, providing for your children, and ensuring that you don't have to spend your retirement years subsisting on cat food.

By this measure, Andrew Swann is a superstar among individual investors. Andrew, his wife Rosemary, and their dog and cats live in an expansive home in the hills of San Miguel de Allende in Guanajuato, Mexico. Their yard is adorned with peach, pecan, palm, and pear trees. A large agave cactus sits outside Andrew's sun-drenched office. The Swanns have also built a country home in southern Chile on 50 acres overlooking Panguipulli Lake with spectacular views of snow-covered Villarrica volcano rising 9,300 feet.

Andrew is quite a good doubles player and plays tennis on nearby clay courts three times per week. He also loves to fish, and his wife Rosemary is a painter who has a large studio on their property.

Living in Mexico, the Swanns are understandably private about the amount of capital in the form of real estate, hard assets, and stocks that they have accumulated. Suffice it to say that they can pursue their passions without worrying about Social Security or a company pension plan.

Professional investors like to scoff at gold bugs like Andrew Swann. But Swann is no nutcase with visions of financial Armageddon, hording Krugerrands under his mattress. Swann is more than just an ordinary gold stock investor. Like a private equity investor or investment banker, Swann has become a deal maker. His specialty is uncovering promising junior mining stocks and helping them locate financing so that they can grow. In the process he has made his family very comfortable financially and very happy.

From Detective to Deal Maker

Andrew Swann has spent the better part of the last 15 years learning the ropes of investing in gold stocks and other hard assets. As an individual investor, he not only spends hours researching stocks online, but he also talks to management whenever possible, attends mining industry trade shows and has traveled around the world touring many of the gold mines he invests in.

For investing ideas Andrew, like other individual investors profiled in this book, puts a high value on developing a network of trusted sources and like-minded investors for information sharing.

Besides ValueForum.com Andrew also is a member of a message board called Smart Investment.ca (www.SmartInvestment.ca), which is run by Canadian Mike Kachanovsky. Online, Kachanovsky is known as Mexico Mike because of his fondness for Mexican mining companies. His web site contains information on Canadian-listed junior gold and silver stocks, and has active message boards. Swann also spends time scanning for ideas on InvestorsHub.com and on the Gold, Mining and Natural Resources forums on Silicon Investor.

Swann is a regular subscriber to Eric and David Coffin's *Hard Rock Analyst,* a premium investment newsletter run by two brothers. One brother focuses on the geology behind mining stocks and the other focuses on the finances. Swann also reads *The Ormetal Report.* A French-Canadian named Claude Cormier, whom Swann considers his favorite small-cap gold analyst, produces *Ormetal.*

Strategy Tip

Since many stocks Swann invests in trade on Canadian exchanges, Swann often uses the Canadian equivalent of the SEC web site called SEDAR.com for company filings. Company web sites are also a great source for disclosure documents.

Another newsletter he scans for ideas is the *Speculative-Investor* run by Steve Saville, an Australian residing in Shanghai, China. Swann also checks a number of other gold-oriented sites, including Bullion Vault at www.bullionvault.com, which serves as a good digest for gold market news.

Command central for Swann is a spacious office he built on his land in San Miguel. His office is complete with a satellite-connected flat screen wall television, two big screen Apple iMacs, and a Macbook laptop that he uses for traveling and for video chats via Skype. One of his displays is always devoted to market data, real-time Level II quotes and account data from Stockhouse.com, and from his brokerage firm E*Trade.

Swann spends hours online each day doing his research or detective work, tracking down leads, reading news reports, and trolling message boards. He also visits company web sites for reviewing regulatory filings.

Despite his wired office in the heart of Mexico, Andrew is not the type of investor who becomes chained to his computer for due diligence. His days as a petroleum landman in East Texas taught him the value of a shoe leather and handshake approach to information gathering. Thus Andrew makes it his point to attend precious metals industry presentations and trade shows like the Vancouver Resource Investment Conference held in British Columbia.

Andrew is a big believer in talking to management. For example, one of Andrew's best investments was in a Brazilian mining company called Desert Sun Mining (see Figure 8.2). At the time its main asset was an old mine that had been shuttered because gold was trading at less than $300 per ounce. The low price had rendered production uneconomical.

When Andrew first noticed the stock in 2005, gold was trading at just above $400 and Desert Sun's Jacobina mine had been reopened. So Andrew bought a small amount of its shares.

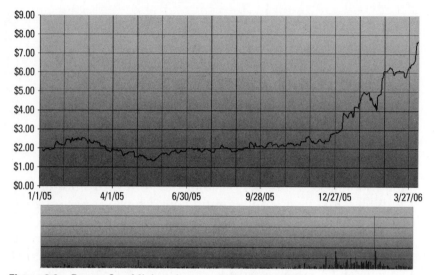

Figure 8.2   Desert Sun Mining, January 2005–April 2006
Source: © TickerTech.com, 2010.

He then noticed that it had gotten a new chief executive by the name of Bruce Humphrey and that the company planned to issue warrants.

So Swann made a telephone call to one of the company's senior officers, John Carlesso, then vice president of corporate development. He asked him what was going on. Carlesso informed Swann that Humphrey had departed from the number two job at one of the world's biggest gold producers, Goldcorp, and was highly sought by other mining companies.

However, after the prospective chief executive had done his own due diligence, he decided to join Desert Sun. "That's all I needed to know," says Swann. "If one of the smartest guys in the business had his pick of the litter, and this is the company that he chose, that gave me an incredible amount of confidence."

So after the company issued warrants in a private placement, Swann bought a large amount of them as they became available on the market. His initial price was $C0.35 per warrant, well below its stated exercise price of $C2.50.

Flush with capital from issuing warrants, Humphreys continued to expand Desert Sun's asset base and then eventually he sold the entire company to Yamana Gold for approximately $8 per share.

The warrants, which leveraged the movement of the common stock, rose to more than $4 each. It was one of Swann's first 10-baggers.

The Desert Sun experience taught Swann two very valuable lessons. First, don't be timid about talking to management. Second, if you like a company's prospects, try to obtain warrants, and if at all possible, get involved in the private placements directly.

For most small investors buying into private placements is impossible; however, by pooling their assets together Swann and his network of gold investor friends have been able put together small private placements for junior mining companies. This allows Swann to effectively buy shares at a discount to the going market price.

Some of the mining companies that Swann has assisted in private financings include Quebec-based miner Metanor Resources, Gold-Ore Resources, a junior mining company in Sweden, and Kinbauri Gold Corp., a company with mines in Spain.

Prior to committing to these financings Swann likes to visit the actual mines and arrange to have a tour with management. "Just seeing the functioning mechanics of a gold mine, and going underground, and seeing the veins, and seeing how the rock is drilled and blasted is very useful," says Swann. "It's also important to see what kind of passion management has for these mines."

If there is one financial metric Swann focuses on, it's cash flow. For mining companies, this is essentially a calculation of the cash costs of producing the ore subtracted from the price the company is getting for its gold.

Swann readily admits that he is no financial expert, but he can run screens as well as the next guy and adds that if he doesn't understand something on a company's balance sheet he will consult friends who have more expertise in financial statement analysis.

Swann typically holds about 25 stocks in his portfolio at any given time, mostly gold stocks but also some income-oriented energy

Strategy Tip

Whenever possible Swann avoids OTC Bulletin Board or pink sheet versions of Canadian mining stocks because they lack liquidity and their spreads tend to be higher. Several brokers like E*Trade will allow you to buy Canadian stocks locally in Canadian dollars, so you don't become victim of exchange rate fluctuations and markups.

investments. Of course, Swann has had his share of wipeouts and occasionally he comes across so-called pump and dump stocks where would-be analysts or newsletter gurus are getting paid to endorse a questionable stock.

Two companies Swann invested in—Australian miner GBS Gold and North Sea driller Oilexco—suffered a liquidity crisis in 2008. Swann lost nearly all of his investment in Oilexco. Even worse Swann saw more than 60 percent of his entire stock portfolio melt away as global securities markets and commodities like gold plummeted.

"It was shocking really. I wasn't sleeping well during that period," says Swann. Fortunately he recovered most of his losses when markets and gold recovered. Nowadays Swann limits each investment to no more than 4 percent of his portfolio unless he has done significant due diligence. He also eschews leverage and prefers to keep a small portion in cash at all times. "Dry powder," he calls it.

Who Is Andrew Swann?

Andrew Swann's roots run deep in Tyler, Texas, or as he likes to describe it, "behind the pine curtain," referring to East Texas's distinctly Old South feel compared to the western half of the state. His family founded Swann's Furniture Gallery in 1895 in Tyler, and it remains a retailing fixture in the city. Swann's maternal grandfather, Walter Dossett, co-founded Extraco Bank in Waco, Texas. Swann continues to collect dividends from the bank.

Andrew has a brother who's an attorney in Waco and a sister who is a homemaker in San Antonio. His father, now 83, ran the furniture business for years and sparked Andrew's interest in business and investing. He gave Swann his first shares of stock when he was 14 years old.

After Swann graduated from the University of New Mexico in 1976, majoring in history and economics, he spent a brief amount of time working in manufacturing with his uncle, but then in 1980 a college friend lured him into the oil and gas business.

Swann was recruited to be a petroleum "landman." The aftermath of the fall of the Shah of Iran in 1978 and the Iran-Iraq war sent oil prices soaring. The average price of a barrel of oil rose from $12.64 in 1979 to $34 per barrel in 1980. Rig counts in Texas and other oil states shot up, and lease deals were breaking records.[2]

During these heady days, big petroleum companies like Atlantic Richfield and Conoco employed armies of young men on the ground whose job it was to negotiate and purchase mineral rights on various properties, which could be packaged into oil and gas tax shelters. Former president George W. Bush started out as a land-man, as did the father of billionaire T. Boone Pickens.

"They were just looking for warm bodies because the major companies were trying to put on these huge lease programs and they didn't have enough people to buy the leases," says Swann. So Swann learned to navigate local courthouses and county records to track down landowners. He traveled around in rural areas in Alabama, Arkansas, Louisiana, and Texas negotiating leases.

"It was a lot of detective work," says Swann. "You'd go to the courthouse. You'd read the documents where in 1973 the Jones family sold the land and they retained half the mineral rights. Okay, well, Mr. Jones died, and you'd have to go find his will. He died in 1984, he left it to his three kids, and one of them is dead. So on and so forth."

This kind of detective work would serve Swann well later as an investor performing due diligence on mining companies. Swann gained a hands-on understanding of mineral rights, leases, and most important, the value of assets in the ground.

"It's amazing to me that after 25 years I'm still getting money in the mailbox from that," says Swann referring to the small percentage royalty landmen were sometimes given of the leases they secured.

It wasn't just investigating skills that Swann acquired; as a petroleum landman he also learned how to negotiate. "I loved the detective work in the courthouse and all that, but then you had to go out and meet these people. You had to track them down, and call them on the phone, and go out and sit on the tailgate and drink beer or shoot doves with them; whatever it took. We did a lot of dove hunting back in those days," says Swann with a slight East Texas twang.

But it wasn't just small-time farmers that Swann learned to negotiate with. In Stuttgart, Arkansas, Swann negotiated and bought leases from one of *Forbes* magazine's richest Americans, Frank Lyon, business partner of Sam Walton and former owner of a large Coca-Cola bottling operation.[3]

"It was a huge duck-hunting deal, but it was like $10 an acre. I'm writing these guys a check for like $100,000, and I'm so new to this business, and I'm going, 'Is a lawyer going to check my title work?' But it was fast and loose, and it was a great learning experience."

Swann prospered with the industry and made enough money to pay off his 15-year mortgage within three years. By 1986 as crude oil prices fell,[4] business slowed for Swann. He had to figure out what he would do next.

He tried working in his family's furniture store for nine months but didn't like sales. So Swann headed to San Miguel de Allende, Mexico, a picturesque colonial town in the mountains of central Mexico. He had remembered visiting there as a boy and falling in love with the place. His plan was to take six months off, learn Spanish and figure out whether to go to law school. It was 1987, and Andrew was 32 years old.

"I was walking from my hotel on a cobblestone street, down the hill into San Miguel, and I just had this epiphany," says Swann. "This big voice in my head said, "You dumb ass, why don't you just live here if you like it so much?" So Swann went home to Tyler and told his wife Rosemary that they should sell everything and move to Mexico. "It took her about three seconds, and then she said, 'Let's do it,'" says Swann.

Turns out that Swann moved to San Miguel de Allende, Mexico, at an opportune time. San Miguel de Allende was founded in 1542 by Franciscan monks and is regarded as one of the birthplaces of Mexican independence. Historically it was an important stopover on the "silver" route from Zacatecas to Veracruz, and in 1926 the Mexican government declared the architecturally rich Spanish colonial town a national historic monument.

The charming city is now a center for art and culture, including a prestigious international film festival and several art schools. There are also numerous hot springs in the area. It is a popular tourist spot for those living in Mexico City, and in recent years it has seen an influx of Americans, Europeans, and South Americans.

"Our idea was we were going to move to Mexico for one year, and then go back and maybe I would attend law school. But we just never left. We fell in love with Mexico, and I found that there were so many more business opportunities here," says Swann.

In fact, soon after the Swanns arrived in Mexico they teamed up with a partner, bought some land in the hills with a view of the town and built a spec house on the extra lot. They sold the small house for 100 percent profit almost immediately. "We said, geez, this could be a business," says Swann.

So for the next several years Swann, his partner, and a Mexican architect teamed up to build homes. They sold them to Californians, Texans, and others who were flocking to San Miguel during the 1990s.

Says Swann, "They would walk into these houses with a beautiful view over this colonial city and see orange and palm trees, and this wonderful paradise. And they would say, 'You know, if this house was in California, it would be a $1.5 million, and all you want is $450,000.' And we'd go, 'That's right.'"

Swann managed the books and spent a few hours a day visiting the building sites; the rest of the time he spent monitoring his portfolio, playing tennis, and reading up on economy history. In 1996 Swann started taking an interest in gold.

"It became apparent to me that the price of gold was too low for the amount of money that was being created. When Nixon closed the gold window, we entered into a new world where there was no currency backed by metal, which had been the case in history until then," says Swann.

Swann then began buying gold stocks–mostly South African miners like Harmony Gold. "I got an incredible education about the gold mining business," says Swann, who says he didn't earn much those first few years investing.

By 1998 Swann quit the homebuilding business and began investing full-time, mostly in gold and oil and gas stocks. Then a few years later in January 2002 Swann read *Tomorrow's Gold, Asia's Age of Discovery*, a best-seller by Swiss economist Marc Faber sometimes known as Dr. Doom.

The book, which predicted the boom in commodity demand from emerging Asian markets, struck a chord with Swann. "It just made so much sense to me because it was, basically, what I had been thinking, and here was somebody who was a lot smarter than I am who was basically saying exactly what I'm thinking," says Swann.

After reading the book, Swann sold off all of his mutual funds and devoted his full-time attention to investing in gold and oil and gas, the commodities he figured China would be consuming in large quantities.

Andrew devoted much of his time each day to researching stocks and discussing ideas online. Along with a few dozen other investors that he met online on an old Yahoo message board, Swann joined the premium stock picking community ValueForum. He was the 42nd member of what is now a community of nearly 1,200 members.

"I had some doubts about joining a pay site, but it turns out that it was just fantastic because it eliminated a lot of the brouhaha that goes on at most sites," says Swann referring to the other smart investors he met on ValueForum and low tolerance for touting in the community. Swann learned about investing in Canadian energy royalty trusts, which had generous yields from 15 percent to 20 percent.

Swann, or Swannmex, as he is known to other ValueForum members, quickly became regarded as the resident gold expert, sharing his "Goldspeculatorsportfolio" with other members. In terms of ratings, Swannmex gets the highest possible gold star rating from other members of ValueForum.

The Swanns have benefited so much from Andrew's investing success that at 55, he no longer needs to worry about working for a living. His wife Rosemary has an art studio on their land, and her paintings appear in a local gallery in San Miguel, as well as one in Elgin, Texas. Andrew splits his time between investing, reading, and tennis. The Swanns both enjoy their garden, two cats, and new puppy, Penna.

The couple can also afford to indulge in long adventurous vacations. For the last five years Andrew has spent about a month each year walking 400 miles from Southern France to the Cathedral of Santiago de Compostela in Galicia, Spain–a medieval pilgrimage route that runs through the Basque countryside. Swann is not a Catholic but does consider himself a spiritual person. He and his wife have built a chapel for meditating on their San Miguel property.

And if their life in San Miguel weren't enough of a fantasy, they recently built a home in Chile nestled in the mountains overlooking Lake Panguipulli.

Strategy Tip

Swann buys gold mining stocks but doesn't trust ETFs like SPDR Gold Trust (GLD), where there is ongoing debate among gold bugs about whether there is sufficient physical gold backing its shares. Swann does own physical gold.

"The area we are in Chile would probably be like the way Lake Tahoe was in 1940, before it was developed at all. The roads are still gravel roads. It's like stepping back in time, totally unspoiled and really beautiful," says Swann who plans to spend about four months each winter in Chile.

However, Swann's Chilean real estate is more than just an ideal winter retreat; Swann is worried about America. "I'm extremely concerned about the macro economy in the United States and, by proxy, Mexico. So, my home in Chile would kind of be a place to escape to if things got strange."

Swann predicts gold will ultimately reach at least $3,000 an ounce over the next three to five years.

Swann's Rules of Investing

- **Don't invest in gold stocks—especially junior miners—unless you are prepared for extreme volatility and losses.**

  According to Swann, half of the battle is to identify the big trend (as in "gold is in a long-term secular bull market"). If you have patience and you are right, the bull market will bail you out of 80 percent of your mistakes. Says Swann, "Gold stocks are extremely volatile, so you have to have a cast-iron stomach for the volatility, and you MUST have patience."

  Swann recommends committing 60 percent of the funds you are allotting to gold in long-term core holdings where you have done your homework and 40 percent to taking advantage of trading opportunities. "I wish I were better at this," says Swann.

  Swann adds that most people are much better off buying an ETF like Market Vectors Gold Miners ETF (NYSE: GDX) or Market Vectors Junior Gold Miners ETF (NYSE: GDXJ).

- **Do your own due diligence before committing significant amounts of capital.**

  Says Swann, "Small investments are one thing, but if you are going to take a meaningful position, leave no stone unturned." In junior mining companies where there are few gatekeepers, Swann makes it a point to talk to management and if possible visit the project or mine. "You can get a real feel for management after a 30-minute conversation," says Swann.

- **Avoid leverage and set aside cash.**

  Swann says that this is especially true with volatile gold mining stocks. "Leverage will kill you. I took a terrific hit in 2008, and if I had been on margin I would have been wiped out. As it was I held on, lived to fight another day, and recouped most of my losses in 2009," says Swann, who says he now keeps at least 15 percent cash as "dry powder." "I sleep better and have buying power if there is a real puke out," he says.

- **Ride the coattails of smart people.**

  Swann is a big believer in following the smart money into investments whenever possible. One of his early winners among junior gold stocks was a company called Wheaton River Minerals, a Vancouver-based mining company that had gold mining assets in Mexico, Argentina, and Australia.

  In late 2002 when Andrew first noticed the company, it had proven reserves of more than four million gold equivalent ounces and another four million of inferred resources. Its production costs were $130 per ounce, while gold had risen from about $320 per ounce in the middle of 2002 to a $415 by the end of 2003.[5] Swann discovered that two successful Canadian mining industry moneymen, Frank Giustra and Ian Telfer, were behind Wheaton River, which had been quietly buying up small gold mines in Mexico. That was good enough for Swann. After doing some research, he bought shares in Wheaton and ultimately quadrupled his money by the time Goldcorp acquired the company in 2004.

- **Only invest in things you understand.**

  "If you do not understand how a company makes money, do not invest in it. Period," says Swann.

- **Seek out special situations.**

  Swann points out that most investors have very little patience. This creates opportunities and rewards those who do have patience. "I look for value and try to have the patience to wait for the company to execute its plan," says Swann.

- **Cut your losers when they fail to execute.**

  Swann says this is one of his most difficult rules, especially when he has developed a personal relationship with management.

  "There is a fine line between patience and being stubborn. That line is often *very* hard to discern. There is a tendency to become attached to a company and not make objective decisions."

Swann also points out that no matter how much due diligence you do in the junior gold mining sector there will be investments that are losers. "The good news is, the occasional 10 bagger more than makes up for all the losers," says Swann.

Case Study: OceanaGold (TSE: OGC.CA)

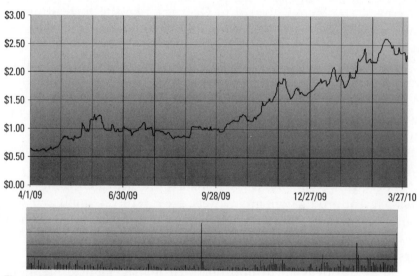

Figure 8.3 OceanaGold, April 2009–March 2010
Source: © TickerTech.com, 2010.

Melbourne, Australia–based OceanaGold Corporation (see Figure 8.3) operates New Zealand's largest gold mine, known as Macraes. It also owns gold and copper development projects in the Philippines. In 2009 the company produced about 300,000 ounces of gold from its New Zealand mines. Its stock is listed on the Australia and New Zealand stock exchanges as well as the Toronto Stock Exchange. It trades over the counter in the United States on the OTC: Bulletin Board or "pink sheets" despite the fact that its market capitalization as of the spring 2010 was $500 million.

Swann first heard about OceanaGold in May 2009 while trolling the investment boards on Mexico Mike's SmartInvestment.ca. He learned that OceanaGold had two big mines in New Zealand

and was producing gold at a cash cost ranging from \$425 to \$475 per ounce.

Swann also learned that the stock was being ignored because most of its gold production had been hedged (meaning, they had presold it) at fixed prices ranging from \$550 per ounce to \$750 per ounce, severely impairing the profitability of the company. This was a consequence of its bankers forcing OceanaGold to enter hedges in order to secure financing for capital expenditures.

This was a "special situation" that Swann thought he should investigate. So Swann headed to Oceana's web site to read up on the company and verify the information he was hearing on the message boards using company documents.

He then compared OceanaGold's predicament to that of another mining company he had invested in called Semafo Inc., a West African mining company that had similar reserve and gold production attributes. It also had been stuck in unprofitable hedged-gold positions, but after it unwound them and was able to take advantage of the much higher spot gold prices, its cash flow and stock soared.

"Well, this company, Oceana, had the exact same thing—dirt cheap, great production, great assets, great reserves, good management," says Swann. "I'm thinking that, if I just have a little patience, this thing is going to be a monster deal, and it ought to be valued at least as well as Semafo, which would mean at least \$5 per share."

So Swann decided to find out what management's intentions were regarding financings and these hedge contracts. After poring through company documents and presentations online, and conversing with management, it became clear that OceanaGold's management was eager get out of its hedges as soon as possible.

Swann went to work creating a model to figure out what OceanaGold might be worth. He calculated fully diluted shares and then estimated what the company would bring in if it could get about \$1,000 per ounce for the 280,000 ounces of gold it could produce in 2010, unhedged. He subtracted out a \$475 as its cash cost per ounce and then figured out what Oceana might trade for based on a cash flow per share figure.

"These companies were selling on average at about 11 times free cash flow. I modeled Oceana, and I realized that, once the hedges were gone, they were selling at about four times free cash flow," says Swann. Swann then proceeded to buy a major stake in the Toronto-listed shares of OceanaGold at prices ranging from $C0.95 to $C1.15.

Swann also liked the fact that the company had acquired an excellent copper and gold mine in the Philippines that he thought could eventually add another 120,000 ounces of gold to Oceana's production, with its copper production paying for most of the costs of development of the mine.

On March 31, 2010, OceanaGold announced that it had successfully closed out all of its hedging facilities and that its cash flow would increase by 200 percent for the remainder of 2010. Said CEO Paul Bibby, "The elimination of hedged contracts is transformational for OceanaGold." By then Swann was already sitting with a 100 percent return on his initial Oceana investment and was expecting its stock to double again.

Swann
In His Own Words

On Owning Physical Gold

I buy physical gold today because it's really money and it can't be created out of thin air by a politician, or by a bureaucrat, or a banker. It has real value, as it has had for 6,000 years.

—*March 2010*

On Whether He Is a Speculator or Investor

I often say, "this is speculating, not investing," but the fact is this is a particular type of investing, and as long as your basic premise holds (i.e., that gold is in a long-term secular bull market) and as long as you are willing to do copious amounts of research and due diligence, then you are speculating with a distinct edge and that has proven over the last eight years to be *very* profitable.

—*March 2010*

On Living in Mexico

When I'm in the United States I feel like I'm swimming upstream, and when I'm in Mexico I feel like I'm laying on my back floating downstream. I've just always loved Mexico, the people, the culture, the beauty.

—*March 2010*

Stock Angler

Investor: Justin Uyehara

Date of Birth: February 13, 1970

Hometown: Elk Grove, CA

Personal Web Site: None

Employment: Engineer, state of California

Passions/Pursuits: Fishing, Sacramento Kings

Investment Strategy: Active trend trading

Brokerage Accounts: E*Trade, TD Ameritrade, Charles Schwab

Key Strategy Metric: Percentage Gainers, relative strength

Online Haunts: www.marketocracy.com, www.bloomberg.com, www.thestreet.com

Best Pick: Sunrise Senior Living, Up 92 percent

Worst Pick: Kodiak Oil & Gas, Down 65 percent

Performance Since January 2003: Average annual return of 33 percent versus 6 percent for the S&P 500[1]

W hen Justin Uyehara was a teenager one of his favorite pastimes was fishing. Especially fishing for salmon on the American River not too far from where he lived. Northern California's American River runs from the Sierra Nevadas through the capital into the Sacramento River and eventually out into the San Francisco Bay. Justin's best fishing spot was at the Nimbus Dam in Folsom where there was a hydroelectric plant. Fishing at Nimbus always yielded the greatest catch.

"All of the fish go up the river but they get bottle-necked by the dam," says Uyehara, reminiscing about a 30-pound salmon he landed at age 15.

Most experienced anglers in the Sacramento area know about the salmon at Nimbus. The water is turbulent by the dam, and the large salmon returning from the sea to spawn up river congregate there.

It's a perfect spot for landing big fish, and for youngsters like Uyehara it didn't take a lot of angling knowledge, gear, preparation time, or boating skills to land keepers. Just attach some sardines to your hook, drop your line in, and stay alert.

In some ways the manner in which Justin Uyehara approached fishing at Nimbus Dam resembles the way he now approaches stock investing. Correction: stock trading.

Justin Uyehara does not consider himself an investor. He is a trader. Justin doesn't get bogged down analyzing the fundamentals of a stock, figuring out its intrinsic value or checking its P/E or even plotting out technical patterns on a chart. Justin fishes for keepers by dropping his line among the stocks in the news, typically those caught in a bit of turbulence.

Some of Justin's trades last only a few hours, some a few weeks at most. Long-term values don't interest him. Justin cares more about what he might be hearing on CNBC or what the price action and volume are in the stocks on his watch list. Justin's most important tools are his Level-II trading screens from E*Trade and his ability to rapidly turn news events into actionable trades. In fact Uyehara's portfolio turnover amounted to a whopping 3,736 percent for the year ending March 31, 2010. Compare that with Chris Rees, the deep value investor profiled in Chapter 1, whose portfolio turnover was 59 percent.

Unfortunately, Justin doesn't have as much time for angling anymore. He spends about five hours each day, before and after his work as a structural engineer for the California Department of Transportation, trading his portfolio. He loves buying into stocks that are big gainers or shorting big losers, and he doesn't stick around in the stocks long enough to care about any one of them.

Justin has had some great winners, including Citigroup (NYSE: C), which he traded in and out of all through 2009. So far he has amassed more than $500,000 in gains from volatile Citi alone for his virtual fund. According to Marketocracy, Uyehara has made money on 68 percent of the stocks he has ever traded. When he is right about a stock, he makes two times as much as he loses when he is wrong.

Even more impressive is how he nimbly was able to avoid getting clobbered during the 2008 market downturn. During that year Uyehara's portfolio return was an impressive –1 percent versus –37 percent for the S&P 500.

Since joining stock picking community Marketocracy.com in January 2003, his average annual return through March 31,

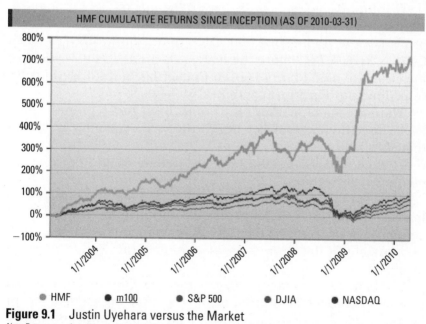

Figure 9.1   Justin Uyehara versus the Market

Note: Returns are after all implied fees including 5c/share transaction fees; SEC fees; management and administration fees of 1.95 percent.

Source: Marketocracy.com; data as of March 31, 2010.

2010, has been 33 percent versus 6 percent for the S&P 500 (see Figure 9.1). Uyehara's alpha is an impressive 25 percent—meaning Uyehara has outperformed the market by 25 percent on average for the last seven years.[2] Had you invested $100,000 in Justin Uyehara's virtual mutual fund (HMF) on Marketocracy.com in January 2003, it would have been worth $776,000 as of March 31, 2010.

Do as I Do, Not as I Say

Of all of the outstanding investors in this book Justin Uyehara's methods for picking winning stocks may be the most difficult to pin down.

When you ask Justin how he does it, his responses are flippant. "I just go with my gut, follow the trends." Press him for specifics, and he might offer up some hints about how he checks for big gainers and big losers each night after the market closes. He also will admit that he likes to trade on earnings announcements ("I get busy during earnings season") and might check relative strength stats. But that is about as deep as it gets with Justin Uyehara.

If you press him for his analysis of the market, he will immediately start offering up the kinds of sound bites he hears on some of his favorite trading-oriented cable shows. Justin likes to watch CNBC's *Squawk Box* before the market opens and *Fast Money* after the close. He used to be a big Jim Cramer fan and still devours his subscription to TheStreet.com's Real Money web site.

Here are some market predictions from Justin given in June 2009, just after the market began the steep rebound it started that March:

"I think we will just be in a big trading range. Probably go nowhere, maybe down."

Uyehara then waxed on about politics and how it was ruling the market. "If the government wrecks the currency, the market could go up," said Uyehara. "If they give everyone money, like hundreds of thousands of dollars and just print money, the market could go up a lot."

Uyehara was presumably referring to how government stimulus packages were artificially propping up the economy and market. To be sure, some economists might take issue with Uyehara's economic theories and the idea that inflation and a debasement of the dollar would be bullish for stocks.

Strategy Tip

Level II quotes give traders real-time access to market makers' bids and offer prices. For Uyehara they offer demand and supply insights into who and what might be driving a stock's price action. He gets in-depth market quotes through his Power E*Trade Pro account.

But they would be missing the point. It's not important to listen to what Justin is actually saying about market direction, politics, or the economy. From an investment standpoint, it is more important to watch the moves Justin makes in his portfolio.

Justin is a trend trader who has 100 stocks on his watch list and frequently makes more than 20 trades per day. If Justin didn't have to go to work at 9 A.M. Pacific Time (two and a half hours after the market opens in New York), Justin admits that he would be a full-time day trader. In the stock market, day traders are known for rapid trading, taking advantage of volatile stocks and wide bid-asked spreads, and selling out all of their positions by the end of the day.

Real-time quotes are a necessity for these traders, and because Uyehara is such an active trader he has a Power E*Trade Pro account. This gives him access to Level II quotes on NASDAQ and OTC Bulletin Board stocks. He also gets sector data, a live stream of CNBC, and can direct his trades to ECNs like ARCA that often fill orders faster.

"I trade for the first few hours of each day before I go to work, try to make a few hundred bucks. Then I'm out," says Justin, who tends to hold stocks longer for his Marketocracy portfolio because of the web site's stringent rules. "I enjoy [trading], it's not like work to me."

Uyehara cares little about company fundamentals or the Federal Reserve's dollar policy and their affect on specific trades. He just wants to know what stock tickers are moving and if it's prudent to hitch a ride on a particular trend. This is not to say that Uyehara is ignorant of macro and fundamental forces affecting the stocks because his "gut" trading demonstrates an implicit understanding of many fundamental practices like contrarian buying (he looks for market overreactions) and technical practices (he checks relative strengths).

Strategy Tip

Relative strength is a technical measure of how a particular stock's price is trending relative to the sector it belongs to. An RSI or relative strength index of 70 or higher means a stock is overbought and below 30 is oversold.

"One key to my style is to just be quick in identifying trends. For example, if I see companies selling off on good news, then I might become more cautious on the market and on all my stock selections," says Uyehara. He points out that this was happening in the first few months of 2010. During that time Uyehara traded in and out of many ultrashort sector exchange-traded funds.

If Justin is wrong about a bet he makes, he nimbly sells out and either reverses course or moves on to the next stock on his watchlist. That is what traders like Uyehara do. They have no allegiance to a particular stock like Intel or Google, and they are not known for sticking to any fundamental or technical bets. They are about the market, the here and now, and they go with the flow.

Here is an example of a typical trade Uyehara entered into in early 2010. On Wednesday, February 11, 2010, before the market opened, Emeryville, California's LeapFrog Enterprises (NYSE: LF) announced strong fourth quarter earnings of $0.46 up $1.14 from a loss, blowing away analysts' estimates. Soon after the announcement, articles appeared on Reuters.com, Bloomberg.com, and on TheStreet.com mentioning that LeapFrog shares were rallying on above-average volume.

Uyehara acted quickly and purchased 120,000 shares of LeapFrog in four separate trades for his Marketocracy fund at prices from $4.50 to $4.74. The stock closed that day at $4.77 on volume that was nearly 16 times the volume it had the day prior to its earnings announcement. Checking his Level II quotes, Uyehara saw that the volume continued to be heavier than normal for the remainder of the week. The buyers were still supporting the stock, and its price held steady at about $4.70. That was a good sign.

However, by the following Tuesday LeapFrog shares had inched up over $5 to an intra-day high of $5.40 (see Figure 9.2). That was good enough for Uyehara. He sold the bulk of his holdings

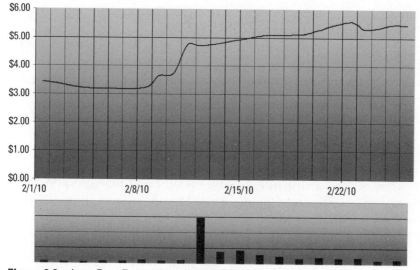

Figure 9.2   LeapFrog Enterprises (NYSE: LF), February 2010
Source: © TickerTech.com, 2010.

at $5.20. After commissions that gave Uyehara about a 10 percent return in less than a week on LeapFrog.

That same Tuesday, February 17, Uyehara bought and sold 6,000 shares of offshore driller Transocean Ltd. (NYSE: RIG) in a single day. After commissions he netted a $0.69 or $4,140 in profit.[3]

But don't bother asking Justin about why he chose Transocean or LeapFrog. He is not likely to remember the trades. In fact, from the time he started his portfolio on Marketocracy in January 2003 through March 31, 2010, Uyehara has made a dizzying 6,239 trades turning over 90 million shares. An impressive 68 percent of his closed positions have been winners, and his average annual return has been 33 percent.

Believe it or not, Justin says he is trading more frequently in his personal discount brokerage accounts, where he also engages in short selling and leverage. Uyehara's long-only Marketocracy fund prohibits buying on margin and short selling.

In November 2004 Uyehara created a short-only virtual mutual fund on Marketocracy.com (Marketocracy offers long-only or short-only funds). As of late April 2010 it had an average annual return of 21 percent versus 2 percent for the S&P 500. Its alpha was even higher than Uyehara's long-only fund, scoring 35 percent outperformance relative to the S&P on average.

Of all of the strategies outlined in this book, Justin's is probably the most difficult and dangerous to mimic. Uyehara-style investing requires taking significant risks on what would seem to be little more than gut instincts. Moreover, commissions are a significant factor, as Uyehara has spent more than $4 million in virtual commissions in his seven years trading on Marketocracy.com. And lest we not forget—taxes. Justin trades his real-life E*Trade account hyperactively, and he admits that he gets killed paying short-term capital gains taxes on profits.

Like other successful traders—hedge fund managers Michael Steinhardt and Steven Cohen of SAC Capital for example—Justin Uyehara is somehow wired for it. It is part of his DNA. When he talks about trading by "feel," it's almost as if he were some kind of Jedi master of stock trading. "I feel like I am part of the market. My trades depend on the emotion of the market. If the market is happy, I'm happy," says Uyehara.

Who Is Justin Uyehara?

Justin Uyehara was born in Okinawa, Japan, the third of four children of Japanese-American parents. Justin's father was from Hawaii, but like many other patriotic Japanese immigrants known as *Nisei* he enlisted in the U.S. armed forces (Army Air Force) during World War II. He is 85 years old today.

When Justin was six, his father was transferred from Okinawa to McClellan Air Force base, just outside Sacramento. Justin had a pretty typical 1970s and 1980s California upbringing. He attended Grant Union High School in Sacramento and graduated in the class of 1988.

Justin recalls that he was an average student. He didn't play high school sports, nor was he involved in clubs or the school band. Justin liked to go fishing for salmon and striped bass, and he collected fishing lures.

Justin had little preference for what he wanted to major in after high school, so he figured that since his older brother majored in electrical engineering he might as well also. He picked civil engineering and went to Cal State, Sacramento, living at home and working at a local Kmart store. After graduating in 1995, Uyehara went to work for a small private engineering and construction firm.

It was about this time that Justin started investing. All he knew was that he wanted to make money and he liked the idea of the stock market.

Those were the heady days of the Internet and tech stock craze, and it didn't take Justin long to open up an online trading account with DLJ Direct (now part of E*Trade). Like many others at the time, Uyehara began to teach himself about investing by going online and watching CNBC. He became a fan of two market pundits, The Chart Man, Gary B. Smith, formerly of TheStreet.com, and contrarian money manager and columnist Bill Fleckenstein, who often wrote for MSN's Money Central site.

Eventually Justin landed a better job working for the State of California as a structural engineer, but he continued to pursue his passion for trading. When asked whether he was burned during the Internet bubble's bursting in 2000, Justin replies that his brokerage account was small at that time and that once he saw the market falling he sold out, limiting his losses.

In 2003 Uyehara discovered Marketocracy.com, and since he always had aspirations of managing money full-time, he thought its proposition of finding the best-performing unknown money managers was compelling.

Today Uyehara lives with his wife and stepdaughter outside Sacramento, and he spends most of his free time investing or following his favorite team, the Sacramento Kings. Uyehara is part of Marketocracy's mFolio money management program but that offers him relatively little income, so he is still devoted to his government job.

California's recent fiscal woes mean that Uyehara has had three furlough Fridays every four weeks. That is just fine by him. He wakes at 5 A.M. to begin his market day online but typically has to cut it short to go to work at 9 A.M. He enjoys trading, so three more days attending to his portfolio is his pleasure.

Uyehara's Rules of Investing

- **Above all, be flexible.**

    Uyehara is never dogmatic about sticking to any bullish or bearish convictions he might develop about the market. He trades the trend.

    "Sometimes I'm in and out of a stock. The most important thing is to be flexible. Nothing is set in stone, everything varies," says Uyehara.

In early 2010, for example, he believed that the market was "getting toppy." This made him nervous, and he put in place several inverse index ETFs as hedges. However, this didn't preclude Uyehara from riding earnings stocks or rallying stocks.

On March 2, 2010, for example, Uyehara read the news that Ethan Allen Interiors (NYSE: ETH) orders were up 25 percent. The next day its stock opened at $18, up $2 from the previous day's close. Uyehara acted fast and bought 30,000 shares at $19.18 and sold at $19.93 the same day. After commissions he netted $22,500 in his Marketocracy portfolio.

- **Listen to what the market is telling you.**

When Justin Uyehara talks about The Market he truly refers to it in the same way that Benjamin Graham did, as a living breathing being, Mr. Market. One factor Uyehara keys in on is sector trading action. For example, in April 2010, Uyehara began to sense that the market no longer liked health care because he began to see stocks trade lower, even when the news was good.

For example, on Monday April 26, 2010, Humana (NYSE: HUM) reported a 26 percent surge in its first quarter profit, yet its stock fell from $46.92 to $43.56. Said Uyehara, "Right now if good news comes out on a health care stock, it will probably go down. Just look at how the price behaves. To me it means that someone big might want to get out. Institutions might be lightening up and moving over to a more cyclical sector as the economy gets better." Thus Uyehara might be inclined to short health care stocks as they report earnings or seek out cyclical sectors where institutional money is flowing.

- **Sell Rule: "Don't get too greedy."**

Ask Uyehara what his sell rule is and he is likely to reply, "I usually sell too soon." He adds, "I don't hold anything too long. This limits my gain but also limits my loss."

In fact, Uyehara will not be pinned down to any sell discipline on any stock. As a trader, he goes with his gut and is in and out so quickly he almost never is exposed to the full appreciation or decline in the price of any stock holding. Many of Uyehara's trading gains amount to fractions of a point per share.

Says Uyehara, "That is why I never have a truly big homerun; it is because I never hold on to things too long."

The only exception to this rule has more to do with the fact that Justin is limited to active trading during the hours before he goes to work in the morning. If he has to go to work and has a big position open, he will use a stop-loss to safeguard against big losses while he is busy at work.

"I try not to have one position too big to destroy my account," says Uyehara.

Case Study: Medivation (NASDAQ: MDVN)

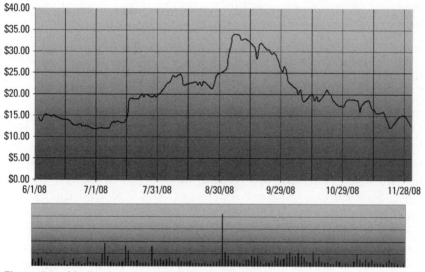

Figure 9.3   Medivation, June 2008–December 2008
Source: © TickerTech.com, 2010.

As a hyperactive trader, Justin Uyehara specializes in exploiting trends in stocks by acting quickly and shaving off fractions of a point in profits from many stocks. Add them all up, and his overall returns are outstanding, despite significant commissions and virtually all short-term capital gains and losses.

One of Uyehara's most successful trades occurred in biotech hopeful Medivation (see Figure 9.3), which Justin has been trading in and out of for years. Not all of Uyehara's trades in MDVN have been profitable but on July 8, 2008, during Justin's regular scan of big price gainers, losers, and earnings news he noticed that Medivation announced the day before that its Dimebon Alzheimer's drug had very positive Phase II study results for patients with Huntington's Disease, a neurological disorder that causes dementia.

Uyehara's quick read on MDVN was good news, and the stock's relative strength was in the 30s, meaning it was technically oversold.

"It caught my attention, and I got into the stock fast. They had some kind of Alzheimer's drug that looked like it really could work," says Uyehara. He was able to buy 20,000 shares of Medivation at $12.26.

While Uyehara often will sell out within a few days, he decided to let MDVN run because it was climbing nearly every day on strong volume at a time when most other stocks were falling due to mounting concerns over the financial crisis.

On August 27, a few weeks after Medivation made another glowing announcement, Uyehara applied his "don't get too greedy" maxim and sold 75 percent of his position for $21.14, providing a 72 percent gain in less than two months.

His timing was good because just a few weeks later the federal government seized Fannie Mae and Freddie Mac and stocks, including Medivation, began a freefall that seemed to get worse as bad news, like Merrill's Lynch's sale and Lehman Brother's bankruptcy hit the tape. (Uyehara was trading in and out of various inverse ETFs, including ProShares Ultra Short S&P 500 ETF during the market selloff.)

A few months later in late November as our panicky regulators were doling out TARP funds, Uyehara picked up 5,000 more shares of Medivation at a distressed price of $14.30. The company continued to issue glowing press releases and finally about three months later in 2009 Uyehara sold out of his Medivation positions at prices from $19.97 to $23.63.[4]

Ironically, while Medivation has been one of Uyehara's most profitable trading opportunities, it became one of Jack Weyland's worst investments (see Chapter 6) after the company surprised Wall Street reporting that Dimebon had abysmal clinical trial results.

Says Uyehara who, unlike value investor Weyland, invested just a few minutes in checking out Medivation, "That drug really looked like it would work but I guess it proved that it does not. Doesn't matter to me, I've been out of that trade for a while."

Uyehara
In His Own Words

On His Goal of Becoming a Money Manager

I hope one day I can be a real-life money manager, but if I do that, I know I would have to really get into it. Visit the companies and know the management. Me, because I don't do that, so I just get in for a trade.

—April 2010

On Price-Earnings Multiples

During earnings season I get very busy. From what I see a lot of these analysts miss earnings. So you never really know what the earnings of a company are going to be. That is why I don't like to look at P/E's so much.

—April 2010

On the Market's Strong Rebound from 2008

It makes me nervous that this great bull market that we have is all based on government intervention. What is going to happen when they get out? This whole thing is based on the government spending money that we don't have.

—April 2010

CHAPTER

10

Bear Market Hero

Investor: John Navin

Date of Birth: February 16, 1950

Hometown: Boulder, CO

Personal Web Site: John Patric Navin (http://johnpatricnavin.blogspot .com)

Employment: Full-time investor, former radio DJ and stockbroker

Passions/Pursuits: Music, blackjack, meditating, and running

Investment Strategy: Technical analysis, Elliott Wave

Brokerage Accounts: Charles Schwab

Key Strategy Metric: Moving averages, resistance and support levels

Online Haunts: www.marketocracy.com, www.stockcharts.com, www.danericselliottwaves.blogspot.com, www.zerohedge.com, www.markettells.com

Best Pick: Rio Narcea Gold Mines, Up 653 percent

Worst Pick: Scripps, Down 93 percent

Performance Since May 2001: Average annual return of 10 percent versus 1 percent for the S&P 500[1]

A decade ago I used to consider technical analysis or "charting" a fool's game. The idea of looking at historical price and volume patterns and trying to predict the future of a stock or the market didn't make any sense to me. It seemed like a lazy way of approaching securities analysis. Instead of taking the time to actually understand a company and to model out its profit potential, why not skip all the number-crunching and due diligence, and just look at price charts, draw trend lines, and see if you can discern a "head and shoulders" or "double bottom" pattern?

Indeed in the hallways of *Forbes* magazine technical analysis didn't get much respect. Like other financial publications, we beat the drum for long-term value investing and fundamental analysis in nearly every issue. Our pages praised the followers of the Graham and Dodd school of securities analysis, men like Warren Buffett and Bill Ruane, as well as others like John Templeton and Philip Fisher. I was always taught that technical analysis was about as useful as reading tea leaves.

However, after I became editor of Forbes Newsletter Group in 2002, I began to pay attention to the long-term track records of the various subscription advisory services available to individual investors. If you look at *The Hulbert Financial Digest's* various lists of the top long-term performers, including its Honor Roll, you will find that technically oriented investment letters like *The Chartist, NoLoad Fund*X*, and *Bob Brinker's Market Timer* all rank highly.

I am not saying that value-investing newsletters don't get high marks from Hulbert's list as well. *The Prudent Speculator*, which seeks low P/E and low price-to-book value stocks, has been a stellar performer. Still my analysis of the newsletter landscape made me realize that technical analysis not only can work, but is very popular among investors. And I'm not just talking about individual investors.

Many major investment houses employ market strategists who use technical indicators to formulate advice for clients. Moreover, mutual fund managers at firms like Fidelity also use technical indicators like "moving averages" in addition to their fundamental securities analysis.

Technical analysis attempts to measure the collective investor psyche, focusing on the psychology of crowds and the cycles of greed and fear. For me it's a bit self-fulfilling because if stock prices reflect demand and supply, and large numbers of people base their actions on certain chart patterns, then by definition these patterns will be predictive. So paying attention to technical indicators makes some sense. John Navin, the outstanding investor profiled in this chapter, is a card-carrying technical analyst.

I first became aware of John at the end of 2008 when Marketocracy .com founder Ken Kam told me about his great long-term track record and how he had successfully avoided devastating losses during the financial meltdown.

Using Fibonacci analysis, Elliott Wave Theory, and other seemingly complicated variables, Navin's portfolio had a 1 percent loss in 2008 compared to a 37 percent loss for the S&P 500. By the end of 2008 Navin's virtual portfolio on Marketocracy (JMF) had an average annual return of 19 percent since its inception in May 2001 versus –2.5 percent for the S&P 500.

What made John an even more compelling interview for this book is that he actually studied Benjamin Graham's approach in the 1970s, reading *The Intelligent Investor* three times and memorizing the basic principles of value investing set forth in the classic.

John Navin liked Graham's book, but somehow he has always been drawn to statistics and probability—the stuff technicians thrive on. In fact, for several years John earned extra money counting cards at blackjack tables in Las Vegas. So it's quite natural that the mathematics of technical analysis would appeal to him.

Charting has worked out so well for Navin that he no longer works a 9-to-5 job in the radio business. He is now investing full time, running his own small hedge fund. Last year was a difficult one for Navin because his technical indicators continued to signify that the strong rebound of 2009 was nothing more than a dangerous bear market rally. John thought it could end abruptly at any time so he stayed bearish, and his track record suffered. As of March 31, 2010, John Navin's long-only Marketocracy portfolio had an average annual return of 10 percent per year since its inception (see Figure 10.1). The S&P 500 return over the same period was only 1 percent per year on average.

Bear Tracking

John Navin's use of charts to guide his portfolio picks has been impressive since Marketocracy began tracking his moves in May 2001. However, what really makes him stand out was his bearish call in 2008.

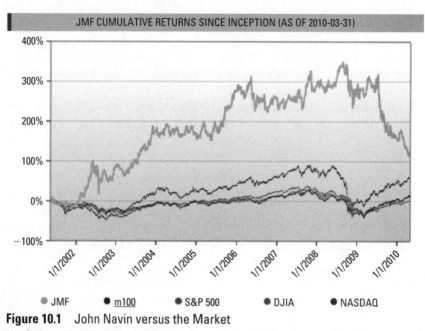

Figure 10.1   John Navin versus the Market

Note: Returns are after all implied fees including 5c/share transaction fees; SEC fees; management and administration fees of 1.95 percent.

Source: Marketocracy.com; data as of March 31, 2010.

"In late spring [2008] I noticed that the 50-day moving average moved downward and moved beneath the 200-day moving average. For me that is a signal that a bear market is about to unfold," says Navin. "It's the first time I had seen a signal that clear. I saw the signal in almost all sectors that I watch. This was a heads up, and I went to as much cash as I could in the portfolio. I also sought out the stocks that would go down the least."

This prescient move allowed Navin to avoid a sell-off that caused most of professional managers to lose 35 percent or more. Navin ended the year down a mere 1 percent.

"It is funny to hear people on CNBC say that you know it's a bear market when it is down 20 percent," says Navin. "I disagree with that. Typically you can tell well in advance if you are following technical signals."

Of course, dissecting how Navin actually makes decisions from chart patterns takes some understanding of the theory behind technical analysis. In its simplest form, chartists forecast future prices

Strategy Tip

Fibonacci series are a sequence of numbers first created by Leonardo Fibonacci in 1202. Each number in the series is the sum of the two numbers preceding it. Fibonacci sequences are said to appear in nature like in flower pedals, but stock chartists like Navin use them to determine support and resistance levels for stock prices.

based on past price movements relying on the fact that identifiable historical patterns tend to repeat themselves.

Navin looks for mathematical relationships in stock pricing. Specifically, Navin examines price charts looking for emerging Fibonacci patterns. Leonardo Fibonacci was a thirteenth-century Italian mathematician who introduced Europe to the Hindi-Arabic numeral system, now known as the decimal system. Fibonacci also devised series of numbers where each number was the sum of the two preceding numbers in the series. For example, 0,1,1,2,3,5,8,13,21,34 are Fibonacci numbers.[2]

Technicians like John Navin focus on something called Fibonacci retracement. These levels are determined by taking two extreme points (usually a peak and trough) on a stock chart and dividing the vertical distance by the Fibonacci ratios of 23.6 percent, 38.2 percent, 50 percent, 61.8 percent and 100 percent. The resulting levels are used to determine lines of support and resistance for stock prices.

One of the characteristics of Fibonacci sequences is that each number in the series is approximately 1.618 times greater than the preceding number. Hence technicians like Navin place great importance on the key Fibonacci ratio of 61.8 percent, which you get by dividing one number in the Fibonacci series by the number following it. If you believe in Fibonacci retracement, you can then figure out what the next level of resistance or support is for a stock or index. The volume and price action at those levels presumably tell you whether a stock will continue in the same direction or reverse its path.[3]

Another important element in Navin's stock-picking style is his belief in Elliott Wave Theory. Ralph Nelson Elliott developed the Elliott Wave Theory in the late 1930s by claiming that stock markets, then thought to be chaotic, traded in repetitive cycles.

Strategy Tip

R.N. Elliott believed that markets had well-defined waves that could be used to predict market direction. In the late 1930s he developed his Wave Principle, which states that stock prices are governed by cycles based on Fibonacci series.

Elliott discovered that these cycles resulted from investor psychology. He believed that there was a "fractal" nature to the stock market.[4] Fractals involve pretty complex math. Simply put, they are structures that repeat themselves infinitely on an ever-smaller scale. Elliott discovered that stocks trade in similar patterns, and he devised a system of examining waves, using Fibonacci numbers as a guide.

John Navin learned Elliott Wave Theory from one of its chief practitioners, Robert Prechter, and writes about it on his own blog. He also spends time on Elliott Wave–dedicated blogs like "the Elliott Wave Lives On" (http://caldaroew.spaces.live.com) and Daneric's Elliott Waves (http://danericselliottwaves.blogspot.com). Ironically these two blogs had diametrically opposed views on the market during 2009 and 2010.

Unlike many of the value investors profiled in this book, Navin employs a top-down approach to stock selection. Using StockCharts .com, he scans the charts of broad indexes each evening—from the S&P 500 and the Russell 2000 to gold, the dollar, and Treasuries. He is looking to get a big picture macro-read on whether to be bullish or bearish.

He then drills into sectors charts. If he finds a sector that has a promising chart, he will then scan the charts of individual stocks in that sector to identify the best patterns. Moving averages are very important to Navin. When the short-term moving average like the 50-day crosses above a longer-term moving average like the 200-day, it is typically bullish for a stock because it indicates positive demand or buying momentum.

Once Navin has identified a pattern that could be tradable in a stock, he checks other technical indicators to see if they confirm the bullish or bearish pattern he sees developing. These indicators include stochastics, moving average convergence/divergence, and relative strength. If everything checks out, he makes a trade.

Strategy Tip

There are dozens of web sites devoted to educating investors in technical analysis. Navin recommends StockCharts.com, which also has excellent tools for charting. Another good site for creating charts is FreeStockCharts.com.

Navin typically makes trades only about twice per week, and he tends to hold positions from three days to three months. He considers himself to be a swing trader, but is not a day trader. "In my world, six months is long term," he says.

For every trade Navin enters into, he figures out support and resistance levels using Fibonacci analysis and doesn't send the order to his e-broker unless he already has established where his stop loss is going to be. Typically he will never allow a single trade to go against him more than 5 percent. This relatively tight stop system has created problems for him.

During 2009's market run Navin's charts told him to be short in anticipation of the continuation of the bear market. He was especially negative on sectors like financials. So Navin made numerous buys of ProShares Ultra-Short Financials ETF (NYSE: SKF) but because of his tight stop levels, kept getting sold out as financials rebounded sharply. Navin accumulated losses of more than $1.3 million in his Marketocracy virtual fund on that ETF alone.

Besides StockCharts.com, Navin is a member of MarketTells.com, a web site that offers up a host of technical and sentiment indicators daily. Since Navin has been a steadfast bear through most of the market's rebound from 2008's falloff, he has become a fan of the permabear blog Zero Hedge, found at www.zerohedge.com.

Navin makes it his point *not* to read the *Wall Street Journal* every day. "It is a fountain of conventional thinking," he says. "The stories you can't miss, I get anyway on the Web. It is the one paper that everyone from Wall Street reads, so from my standpoint it is loaded with propaganda."

There are occasions when fundamentals do creep into Navin's analysis, but they never play a dominant role. For example, back in early 2009, Navin noticed that Citigroup's charts were indicating that it was becoming oversold and could be bottoming. Navin also saw that Saudi Prince Al Waleed had indicated that he was buying at

$5 per share. Paying attention to "smart money" is not something a pure technician would consider relevant, but Navin used it as a "gut check" to confirm what his charts seemed to be telling him.

When making a trade Navin typically asks himself about 25 questions, which are outlined on his Strategy page on Marketocracy .com. The questions range from "Are there any trends indicating candlesticks?" and "Are the oscillators entering into or coming out of an overbought or oversold conditions?" to "Can a clear Elliott Wave pattern be determined?"

In 2002, not long after Navin joined Marketocracy.com, he noticed that the charts for gold stocks were exhibiting a classic five-wave, Elliott Wave pattern. It was a time when gold prices and gold mining stocks were languishing.

"I saw a pattern in the gold and silver index (NASDAQ: XAU), which was a completion of a technical pattern that means the

Figure 10.2   Goldcorp (NYSE: GG), 2000–2003

Comments from John P. Navin: Arrow underneath the price shows the moving average cross. First bullish signal. Arrow above the price (shortly afterward) shows break above previous (year 2000) resistance—a breakout and confirming bullish signal.

Source: Chart courtesy of StockCharts.com.

trend is about to change," says Navin. "The chart was putting in low divergences, and the (Elliott Wave) count looked good." He also noticed that the short-term moving average had crossed above the long-term moving average on good volume.

So Navin made a major investment in gold stocks (see Figure 10.2), starting with big liquid stocks like Goldcorp (NYSE: GG) and Newmont Mining (NYSE: NEM) and then continuing to buy into junior minors, whose financials looked terrible but charts looked promising.

Navin made a killing investing in more than a dozen gold and metals stocks from 2001 through 2007. Two of his most profitable investments were his investment in Goldcorp and another junior miner Rio Narcea Gold Mines. But like Justin Uyehara (see Chapter 9), Navin barely remembers the names of the stocks he bought. It was the charts he was buying into, not the companies' stories.

While his technically driven gold stock call was spot on, his consistent negative view on the stock market since 2008 hurt his performance in 2009. Navin's portfolio was down 33 percent in 2009, a year when an index fund investment in an ETF like the Spiders S&P 500 (NYSE: SPY) would have returned 21 percent.

"It's been a bear market rally. It's classic. If you dropped out the Citigroup volume, it's remarkably low volume. Nonetheless, it keeps going up," said Navin in the spring of 2010 with the S&P 500 at 1216.

"The level I'm watching here is 1230 on the S&P 500. It's one of those retracement levels of Fibonacci analysis. It's like the 61.8 percent retracement from the 1576 high to the 673 low.[5] If it gets beyond that, I'll give up. But until then, I'm establishing short positions and staying with the long dollar positions."

As of April 2010, Navin was sticking to his guns and believed that the bear market rally would end precipitously and imminently. His target price on the S&P 500: 700.

Who Is John Navin?

John Navin learned about the stock market from his father. As Navin remembers it, it was during a family trip to the Bronx Zoo when he was 13 years old. As animals paced in their cages in front of them, Navin's father pulled out his *Wall Street Journal* and gave his son a guided tour of stock market basics.

For Navin, it was a sweet father-son bonding moment, and he came away with an enthusiasm for stocks. So that next Christmas, his father gave him five shares of an oil company stock. It was 1963 just after Kennedy was assassinated, but before the Beatles would land in America playing to 55,000 teenagers at New York's Shea Stadium.

Young Navin held on to those shares (they are framed in his home office today), but music ultimately became the teenager's passion. Navin attended University of North Carolina (where his father had become a law professor) first as a communications major, but then after taking a class with the noted southern philosopher E. Maynard Adams, Navin switched his major to philosophy. Today Navin likes to point out that Legg Mason Value Trust portfolio manager Bill Miller was a graduate student in philosophy at Johns Hopkins University.

At UNC Navin worked part-time as a disc jockey at the local radio station in Charlotte and continued after college spinning Top 40 tunes by artists like Wilson Picket and Aretha Franklin. His on-air name was Bo Matthews, and he was successful enough to get hired as a program director and DJ for a station in Denver in 1978.

During his years as a radio DJ in the 1970s, Navin started getting interested in investing again. He began to read *Barron's* magazine each week and eventually picked up Ben Graham's *The Intelligent Investor* because it had been preached as required reading by a few of the money managers profiled in the magazine. However, because Navin knew so little about finance it took him three rereads to finally understand its core value investing concepts.

By 1980, Navin, then 30, was interested enough in the markets that he decided it was time for a career switch. Money market rates had skyrocketed to over 12 percent,[6] and Navin figured that the best way to learn about investing was to become a stockbroker. So Navin joined Dean Witter's broker training program. Navin thought he would learn great investment strategies, but instead he was indoctrinated into the world of telephone cold calling.

"It was horrible. They would have you come in at night and call people at home off a list," says Navin, who admits he was terrible at it. "I underestimated how much of a sales gig it was."

From Dean Witter, Navin moved to a local Colorado firm Boettecher & Co out of Boulder where he primarily sold municipal bonds. He spent his free time reading up on technical analysis.

"Back in late 1974, I was listening to a talk radio show out of Boston. They had a technical analyst on who said that the stock market was bottoming and that now would be a good time to be 100 percent invested," says Navin. Within months the market started a powerful bull run that sent it up more than 50 percent in less than a year. "He predicted this by studying chart patterns, and I remembered that," says Navin.

So Navin became a student of technical analysis. He read a number of books including those by Elliott Wave practitioner Robert Prechter and *Technical Analysis of Stock Trends*, by Robert Edwards and John Magee.

"I used to spend hours adding up and calculating moving averages on yellow pads. It was before we had computers," says Navin who also says he would sometimes telephone Robert Prechter with his questions about Elliott Wave Theory.

Despite his unwavering interest in the market and in technical analysis, Navin became tired of the brokerage business and moved back to radio in 1984. Eventually Navin moved with his family to Las Vegas to be the morning DJ on the Top 40 FM radio station KLUC.

One day while he was walking through the Green Valley public library, he noticed an entire shelf devoted to books on the card game of blackjack. Navin decided that since he lived in Las Vegas, he would learn to play blackjack and attempt to supplement his income. "It's not gambling," insists Navin. "Remember I had a kid and a wife, and I'm working at a radio station. I didn't have the money to gamble."

So Navin read a number of books on card counting systems, including Lawrence Revere's famous book *Playing Black Jack as a Business* and Dr. Edward Thorp's best-seller *Beat the Dealer*.

"The systems revolve around keeping records, money management, risk management, bet size, position sizing, when to walk away and what kind of conditions are important," says Navin. "I mean Thorp's like the Benjamin Graham of playing blackjack."

So Navin studied the systems and then began visiting casinos before getting to work at 4:30 A.M. for his morning shift. He says playing at quieter hours like 3:30 A.M. was advantageous because it was easier to count successfully if you and the dealer are the only ones at the table.

"You can get a table all by yourself, head-to-head with the dealer. The number of bets per hour is staggering, there's no delay so you get to the standard deviation and probabilities much quicker," says Navin.

Navin was careful not to play for more than 40 minutes and to visit a different casino every night so as not to become recognized as a card counter. Navin also never made big bets. His biggest win was $1,200 one morning after starting with $50. Ultimately Navin was able to supplement his radio income with about $300 per week in blackjack winnings.

Navin's blackjack sideline came to an end in the mid-1990s when he was offered a more senior-level radio position back in Colorado. However, Navin never lost his interest in the stock market and continued to trade as a self-taught technical analyst. In 2001 he discovered Marketocracy.com and began managing a virtual portfolio.

"I thought that if I could do well in this, then maybe I could manage money without having to be a salesperson," says Navin, recalling his days as a broker.

Besides his astute navigation of 2008's asset-crushing bear market, Navin's charts alerted him to become very bullish on gold stocks in 2002. This was a major score for Navin and helped propel him into Marketocracy's elite top 100 investor rankings.

Ultimately Navin's success gave him the courage to quit his radio job in 2007 so that he could devote his full attention to investing. His virtual track record was enough to get him financial backers for a real-life hedge fund. Still, despite his years outperforming the market with his virtual fund Navin has continued to keep the bulk of his retirement funds in professionally managed mutual funds.

"At first, I just didn't want to touch my real money because there wasn't enough of it. Then I just wasn't ready psychologically," he says. "My wife didn't want me to do it either, so I didn't. And I didn't want to talk her into it."

Like others profiled in this book, Navin participates in Marketocracy's mFolio money management program that offers separately managed accounts to individual and institutional investors who want to take advantage of Navin's stock-picking skills.

Navin's Rules of Investing

- **Buy stocks at support levels and sell stocks at resistance levels.**
  Support and resistance levels are determined by technical factors including Fibonacci analysis. Typically, support levels are the prices at which a lot of buyers tend to buy into a stock. The opposite is true for resistance levels, in that stocks have

difficulty rising above these levels. Technicians like Navin look for confirmation of either resistance or support for a stock by examining the price and volume action of the stock at certain levels.

- **Pay attention to moving averages.**

   For technicians like Navin who study historical price and volume statistics, moving averages are a core indicator. Moving averages identify bullish or bearish momentum and help define areas of support and resistance. In general, when short-term moving averages like the 20- or 50-day moving average, cross above a longer-term moving average, like the 200-day, it is a bullish indicator. The opposite is also true.

- **Use sentiment indicators as contrarian tools.**

   Navin pays attention to various market sentiment indicators like AAII's survey of bullish and bearish investor sentiment. He also visits a web site called SentimenTrader.com. Generally too much bullish sentiment would cause Navin to be negative on a stock or index.

- **Follow Elliott Wave Theory.**

   The core of Navin's technical approach applies the Elliott Wave Theory, which he initially learned by subscribing to Robert Prechter's newsletter. Elliott Wave involves complicated mathematics, including Fibonacci numbers and fractals.

- **Avoid story stocks.**

   "Anything that has a fantastic, great story that everybody follows, I hate those stocks—Apple, Google, Research In Motion—I never trade them," says Navin.

- **Don't mess with double short ETFs or if there's too much fine print, avoid it.**

   Like other investors during 2009, Navin was burned badly in inverse and leveraged ETFs. Most of these ETFs settle their underlying securities and contracts daily so some investors seeking longer-term results, like shorting an index of financial stocks, wind up with returns that differ from what they expected. Because Navin was not permitted to short stocks in his long-only Marketocracy portfolio, he was forced to buy inverse leveraged ETFs like ProShares UltraShort Financials to create a negative position. This cost him dearly especially given that financial stocks mostly went up in the latter half of 2009.

- **Use stop losses when stocks sink 5 percent below your purchase price.**

  Like most traders, Navin seeks to control his downside exposure so he employs tight stops. During volatile markets, tight stops can be difficult to manage.

- **Regarding profits: If your trade produces a 25 percent gain, sell one-third of your position. At 50 percent gain, sell another one-third.**

  Perhaps taking a page from his days playing blackjack, Navin is a big believer in taking money off the table when you are sitting on profits.

Case Study: PowerShares DB U.S. Dollar Index Bullish (NYSE: UUP)

Figure 10.3 U.S. Dollar Index Bullish Fund, April 2009–April 2010

Comments from John P. Navin: Note MACD "momentum low" in June followed by steadily rising line (bottom of page, below price chart). Note bottom arrow where MACD line finally crosses above the zero line. Note top arrow where significant moving averages cross.

Source: Chart courtesy of StockCharts.com.

Starting in the summer of 2009, John Navin began to see an interesting pattern developing in the stock chart for the U.S. dollar ETF, known as UUP. The U.S. dollar had been falling against other major currencies since late 2008.

Explains Navin, "Elliott Wave Theory involves counting waves. So in 2009, from summer through winter, the ETF tracking the dollar kept hitting new lows, but the volume was declining."

He also saw that there were negative divergences in the price-momentum oscillators. Oscillators are momentum indicators that show how the current price of a stock or in this case ETF, relates to the high-low price ranges or advanced/decline ratios over a set number of periods.

"It would hit a low in the summertime, and then go up, and then hit a low in October. But the momentum oscillator was higher in October than in late summer, even though it was a lower price. That's a sign that it's beginning to bottom, and it's something I look for," says Navin.

Navin also noticed that a MACD (moving average convergence divergence) "momentum low" in June was followed by a steadily rising line (see bottom of Figure 10.3). In December 2009, this MACD line finally crossed above the "zero" line, and finally the short-term moving average line moved above the long-term moving average line as noted by the second arrow in Figure 10.3.

These bullish signals caused Navin to go long the U.S. dollar ETF starting as early as June 2009. It was one of his most profitable trades during that time period.

Navin
In His Own Words

On Playing Blackjack and Investing

To play blackjack correctly and lessen the house advantage, it's necessary to learn basic strategy and card counting. Dr. Thorp's book, *Beat the Dealer*, is all about this. Technical analysis and money management is quite similar. You use many different indicators to come up with a picture of the market. It's not always clear, but when it is, you have to allow the probabilities to work for you and get the big bets out.

In blackjack, this is keeping your unit size appropriate relative to your bankroll. In trading, it's the same thing; in addition to placing stops and diversifying (when appropriate).

I *never* play blackjack on the Web because the deck shuffling after each hand makes it impossible for counting to work. Also, I like to see the face of the human being who's dealing.

—*April 2010*

On Technical Analysis versus Fundamental Analysis

I feel fortunate that early on I learned from reading Benjamin Graham. I got started that way looking for low P/Es and low price-to-book values. *The Intelligent Investor* is the basis of my knowledge about stocks and the markets. Technical analysis is the core of my work now, but I always have the Benjamin Graham stuff in the background.

There are people who want to divide this up, only use one or the other, but why be like that if I can learn and trade based on both together and it works.

—*December 2008, Marketocracy.com*

On the Goldman Sachs Scandal Fallout

It's very likely that financial reform will be much stronger than previously believed—especially as the details of this case and other similar cases filter out. Matter of fact, I could envision a scenario where the too-big-to-fail banks are required to eventually give up their trading arms. It's even possible that we reach a new environment where breaking up the banks into smaller companies becomes politically realistic.

If you don't think this is possible, consider American history: Teddy Roosevelt broke up Standard Oil even though no one believed he could do it at the time. We may be headed in that direction.

—*April 17, 2010, Navin's blog*

CHAPTER

Legendary Investor Incubators

Ten years ago when I was editor of *Forbes Best of the Web* our job was to review hundreds of investment-oriented web sites. Back then, I was excited by the flurry of activity in the online investing arena. Hundreds of new web sites were created for investors who were going online. Investors were flocking to the Web at first because their discount brokers were offering cheaper commissions for electronic trading. Then they began to go online to use free tools, read news, and monitor their portfolios.

However, being a skeptic as well as a student of the investing legends, from Warren Buffett and John Templeton to Peter Lynch and Jack Bogle, I was concerned that cheap PCs and powerful Web software in the hands of mobs of unsophisticated investors were dangerous things. After all, these great investors taught us the importance of things like patience, intrinsic value, contrarian investing, buying what you know, and keeping costs down. For all its promise and freedom, the Web was developing into a cluttered noisy bazaar of enticing investment sites, chat rooms, tools, and schemes.

Nearly anyone could hang out a virtual shingle and claim to be an investment guru. By 2000 people were beginning to think that beating the market was as easy as setting up an account with E*Trade and clicking away. We all witnessed the consequences of this euphoria when the dot-com bubble burst in mid-2000.

The euphoria may have subsided but the number of investment-oriented web sites continues to grow. The Internet is daunting for even the most experienced investors. Sorting out what sites will actually help you become a better investor from those that could lead you down a path of financial ruin is very difficult.

In this final chapter, I give an overview of some of the sites that I have found over the years to be the most useful for learning about investing. Some are powered by experts, and on others you can learn from experienced individual investors. Some of the sites provide great tools for honing your stock-picking skills, evaluating your strengths and weaknesses, and checking up on your portfolio holdings.

I have devoted a significant amount of attention to a group of web sites I call *responsible* stock-picking communities. On the Web there are no shortage of web sites and message boards where you can discuss ideas with other investors. However, most of the stock chatter on popular sites such as Yahoo Finance, AOL and even parts of Motley Fool is just noise. It's the stuff that can distract you from making sound investment decisions.

Responsible stock-picking communities are web sites where somebody, either the web site administrators or the community itself, hold members accountable for their claims. These are sites where there is some clear way to determine whether the person offering an idea or making a recommendation is actually worth listening to. On many of these sites member performance is tracked, comments are rated, and hype and stock touting are shunned.

Marketocracy (www.marketocracy.com)

Welcome to an investment resource unlike any other!

It takes skill to make money in today's markets. We have expanded the search for skill from Wall Street to Main Street and beyond. We are proud to introduce to you our FirstPerson approach to investing. Every FirstPerson analyst has one thing in common -- a proven long-term track record of outstanding investment performance. Here's how it works.

First, it begins with a global search for analysts who demonstrate outstanding investment performance
For the last eight years, Marketocracy has attracted the finest and largest group of independent analysts anywhere in the world to demonstrate their investment skill by managing a model portfolio. Think you're one of the best? Click here.

Second, each track record is carefully analyzed not only for performance but to understand how it was created.
Time reveals skilled investment analysts. Only those whose performance and analytical skill is verified are signed to research contracts. We selected our FirstPerson analysts from an exceptional bench of 500 contracted analysts. To review the performance of our FirstPerson analysts, click here.

Investment Products
• Mutual Funds
• Separately Managed Accounts
Click Here

Analyst Reports
Independent stock and market reports from analysts with track records to back up their opinions. Click here.

Analyst Portfolio Log In
Already a member? Sign In
Want to become a member?
More Info | Join Us

Important Disclosure
An affiliate, Marketocracy Capital Management LLC, manages mutual funds, hedge funds and separately managed accounts.

I consider Marketocracy to be the premiere incubator of outstanding investors on the Web. Since July 2000, Marketocracy has allowed members to run virtual million-dollar mutual fund portfolios. Founder Ken Kam's big idea was that he would monitor member portfolios on his Marketocracy.com site and determine which investors were the best stock pickers.

Ken is himself an accomplished fund manager. He helped create First Hand Funds in the mid-1990s and eventually ran a $1 billion mutual fund portfolio. However, Ken didn't think you needed an MBA or fancy schooling to be a great stock picker. Marketocracy would tap into the vast pool of unknown talent on the Internet to find people who were experts in different niches and sectors. Kam gave them online tools for improving their investing skills and tracked their performance. His goal was to find the best performers in his community and then use their talent to help him pick stocks for a real-life portfolio. In conjunction with starting marketocracy.com, he started an asset management business and a flagship mutual fund, Marketocracy's Masters 100 (MOFQX).[1]

For thousands of virtual portfolio managers on Marketocracy .com, the lure has been the chance to prove that you have what it takes to be a professional investor. Kam's pledge is that if you can prove to him that you are good enough he will allocate assets to your stock picks and you will be paid a research fee based on his firm's assets under management.

All members on his site are subject to the same rigors of real-life mutual fund managers, including liquidity rules and limits prohibiting one position from representing more than 25 percent of assets. He also charges his fund managers virtual commissions and expenses. The idea is for them to be subject to the same kind of compliance rules that a real SEC-registered fund is.

However, for these wannabe money managers, Marketocracy also provides great tools for analyzing one's strengths and weaknesses as a portfolio manager. Do you have an idea what your "alpha" or "beta" is or which sectors your winning percentage is the highest?

The Marketocracy.com portfolio data is closer to the kind of analytical feedback you would get as a professional fund manager than most other investing sites provide. You can also get stock ideas and learn about investing on its forums; however, members do not get direct access to other members' portfolios and specific stock picks. This prevents copycatting.

Despite his stock picking Web community "front end," Kam's business model is asset management. He is not after clicks or advertising. He wants to build a next-generation money management firm, and he needs to cultivate a group of great-unknown stock pickers that will fuel his funds.

One of the best things about Marketocracy.com is that site membership is free and you can create as many million-dollar portfolios—both long and short—as you like. It's a place where you can go and test your ideas and hone your skills as a stock picker without losing your shirt.

You will note that most of the stock pickers profiled in this book call Marketocracy their home base on the Web. That's because of all the online stock picking communities, Marketocracy.com has been around the longest. I intentionally chose to profile some of its best performers because they have been beating the pros for nearly a decade. To date, more than 70,000 virtual mutual funds have been created on Marketocracy.com. Even if Marketocracy's fund managers are playing with virtual money, the long-term performance records of its top members is impressive in its own right.

ValueForum.com (www.valueforum.com)

ValueForum is not quite as old as Marketocracy.com. It was created in 2003. However, what is impressive about this outstanding investor incubator is the peer learning and idea sharing that goes on daily. Unlike Marketocracy, which is a portfolio-centric site that focuses on performance, ValueForum at its core is a message board not unlike Yahoo or Raging Bull. However, ValueForum charges its members $250 per year for access, so these investors are serious and less apt to tout or flame. It is an extremely cohesive community of investors who make recommendations, share market news and ideas, and teach each other successful investing strategies.

There are no virtual portfolios on this site; these investors are talking about their real-life portfolios. Many of them are retired and investing their savings for income and to improve their lives. A few of its members are professional investors, and others have retired from Wall Street. Most that I have met are passionate about investing. Besides its active forums, which include 125 different topics, the site also offers a host of useful tools for the community.

There is also a stock rating system where more than 1,000 stocks are rated based the opinions of members. The members of ValueForum themselves are ranked by stars according to how valuable their recommendations and comments are to others in the community. Another handy feature is the shared stock portfolios that allow you to see what other members are holding. Group calendars are also popular on the site.

The key to the site's success is that its founders, Adam Menzel and Ben Nobel, pay close attention to what the community members want. Back in 2004 community members complained that the forums were cluttered with line after line of polite new replies saying things like "thanks," so Menzel and Nobel quickly added a comments function that didn't create a new post, but rather added positive and negative replies to the bottom of existing submissions. Group polling where any member can pose a poll to the community is another feature that members requested and got. It is this kind of attention to detail that keeps ValueForum members coming back. Its subscription renewal rate is about 85 percent.

So far ValueForum has about 1,200 members, most of whom visit the site every day. In fact, the group is so cohesive and passionate about investing that more than a few have developed lasting friendships on the site. Once a year a core group of several hundred ValueForum members gather in a resort hotel for an investing seminar called Investfest. At the event they dine together, play golf, and hear presentations on investing topics delivered by experts and other members of the community.

Value Investors Club (www.valueinvestorsclub.com)

Value**Investors**Club.com　　Earn $5000 for your Idea!

HOME　　CONTACT US　　FAQ　　Ticker ⬦ _____　Search

THESE IDEAS ARE 90 DAYS OR OLDER
Click here to setup your 45 day delay account.

This page is temporarily available to guests in an effort to attract applications for permanent membership in the Value Investors Club. A maximum of 250 members will be accepted. As a guest, you will not be able to post ideas or comments on the site. Please see bottom of page for important information. Guest access will end soon, if you would like continued access to our site. Apply Now.

Latest Ideas...

Friday, February 05, 2010
4:37AM Young Poong Paper Mfg Co., Ltd. (006740, $16100.00, $29727mn)　　Rating (2 users)
I recommend a long position in YoungPoong Paper Manufacturing Co., Ltd. (hereinafter "YPP"). YPP is a misunderstood and underfollowed gem. The stoc... by khs824

Wednesday, February 03, 2010
7:21PM Macquarie Atlas Roads Group (MQA, $0.80, $361mn)　　Rating 2.7 (26 users)
All numbers are in Australian Dollars unless otherwise specified MQA is a very interesting option with a publicly traded asset worth almost 14x it... by algonquin222

2:47PM ADAPTEC INC (ADPT, $3.07, $369mn)　　Rating 4.8 (13 users)
Dumpster Diving With Adaptec Overview Adaptec, Inc. was founded in 1981 and has a 29-year history of providing innovative data storage hardware... by pokey351

2:00PM AVATAR HOLDINGS INC (AVTR, $17.60, $200mn)　　Rating (None)
Avatar Holdings might be in the worst possible business in today's economy, they own land and build houses in Florida and Arizona. But, to paraphra... by lys615

Tuesday, February 02, 2010
11:58PM FIRST CITIZENS BANCSH -CL A (FCNCA, $172.00, $1795mn)　　Rating 5.7 (11 users)
First Citizens Bancshares, Inc. - $172/share - Groundhog Day 2010 - Ticker FCNCA/B Over the past few months, I've been migrating my portfolio from... by chuck307

Go to 05/07/10 🗓　　< 1 2 3 4 5 >

Functions...
Earn $5000 for your idea!
Apply Now
Idea Board A-Z

Reports...
› Most Active
› Highest Overall Rated
› Highest Quality Rated
› Highest Performance Rated

Topics...
See All Topics
04/29 Macro-themed hedges/

Value Investors Club (VIC) is an exclusive message board for analytically minded value investors. There is no fee to join but full membership requires you to write two detailed research reports on investment ideas annually, and that you rate at least 20 other member ideas. You can only be accepted into the club if the founders of the site think your analysis is well reasoned using fundamental analysis.

Value Investors Club is the creation of New York City hedge fund manager Joel Greenblatt and his partner John Petry. Greenblatt is also famous for writing investing best-seller *The Little Book That Beats the Market* and for creating his Magic Formula Investing web site. More recently Greenblatt and a partner started

Formula Investing, an online stock advisory service based on Greenblatt's strategy.

Value Investors Club was formed in 1999, with a promise that it would give away $5,000 each week for the best investment idea. According to its founders, more than $1 million has been paid to members for their great ideas. You won't find any real names on the site. Everyone uses screen names perhaps because a large number of members of Value Investors Club are actually professional hedge fund managers, analysts, or money managers.

Many people don't yet have the skills to write the kind of research reports that will get you accepted to Value Investors Club. Still, you can benefit from VIC by registering because this allows you 45-day delayed access to the research-rich site. In the world of serious long-term value investing, information that is 45 days old is usually still valuable. There are plenty of great actionable ideas on this site, even if they are a bit stale.

I recommend scanning Value Investors Club to find ideas and to learn how research analysts go about uncovering value.

Motley Fool Caps (http://caps.fool.com)

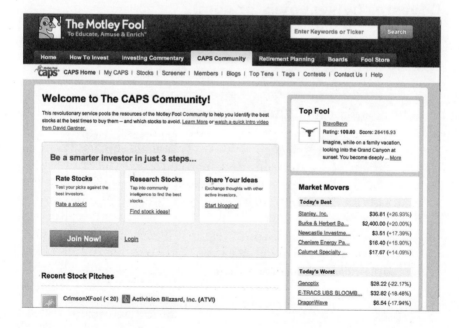

Motley Fool is one of the leading investor sites on the Web. While I will admit to not having spent a huge amount of time on the web site, I know it has gone to great lengths to rate stocks and members. You can use this site to get stock ideas and find members that you think are good at picking stocks. Some have blog posts you can read to help you determine whether you think they are smart. There is also no shortage of useful tools and educational information on the site to help you become a better investor.

Caps' stock pickers rate stocks and some of its top members have more than 200 active stock recommendations at any given time. That's a bit unwieldy and impractical for individual investors in my view. It's also easy to copycat other high-rated members' picks so you need to determine whether the "fool" you are following is the real deal or merely riding the coattails of others.

I recommend using the site's Top Tens tab to quickly find out the best and worst of most of the measurable features on the site. This ranges from those with the highest-rated stock pitches to a list of Hot 5 Star Stocks. A click on "Highest Stock Returns" will yield the members whose average returns are greatest. You will then need to do more digging to find out if the stock picker is worthy of your time.

Covestor (www.covestor.com)

Like the founders of Marketocracy, the people who run Covestor believe that financial services industry professionals from blue chip firms aren't the only smart and talented investors out there who should be your managing money.

Using a Web-based data aggregation technology called Yodlee they invite ordinary investors and financial advisors to link up their real-life brokerage accounts to Covestor's tracking technology. Without divulging specific amounts or your personal account data, the site publishes your holdings and performance record and allows you to blog and comment on stocks. Each Covestor member has a fact sheet associated with him, as well as details about trades and watch lists. The site even tells you who else is tracking each stock picker. This allows you to see if a stock picker's followers are actually making money.

The idea of Covestor is to find smart fellow investors and then track them with a fantasy portfolio. If you like your results, you can then take it to the next level with Covestor Investment Management. CIM will help you create an account with Interactive Brokers that will allow you to auto-trade your brokerage account based on the trades of the stock picker of your choice.

Like Marketocracy, the ultimate goal is to disrupt the mutual fund and professional advice business. The difference here is that the performances of the stock pickers represent real money trades from brokerage account data. Unfortunately, the site is relatively new, and track records don't go back very far. Still, you can learn a lot just by lurking on this site and watching other practitioners.

kaChing.com (www.kaching.com)

kaChing is yet another Web start-up that hopes to turn the established money management business on its head. The site invites Registered Investment Advisors to have their portfolios tracked in order to establish an outstanding performance record. kaChing measures performance and gives each advisor an Investing IQ.

This IQ is based on risk-adjusted performance, how well you stick to your strategy, and the quality of the reasons you give for your trades. The site essentially seeks to match individual investors with the best RIAs so that they can mirror their trades via an account at Interactive Brokers. Minimum account size is $3,000, and the management fee you are charged depends on what the RIA is charging.

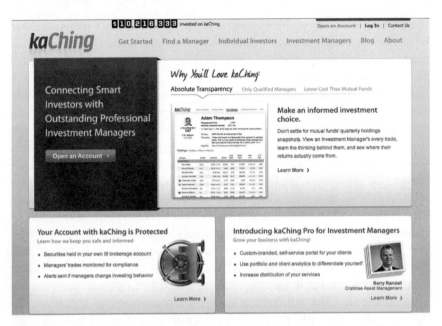

What is useful about kaChing is that it gives you an unobstructed view of how successful investors think and trade. There are also plenty of performance stats and analytics to help you determine which registered investment advisor meets your preferences in terms of investment style and expertise.

RiskGrades (www.riskgrades.com)

The best investors I know understand that you can't have outsized returns without significant risk. Most spend a good deal of their day thinking about what could go wrong with the investment thesis behind the stocks in their portfolio. This free web site was created by some very sophisticated quants formerly of J.P. Morgan. It ranks securities on a scale of 1 to 1,000 according to risk (volatility weighs heavily here). The measure allows you to compare investment risk across all asset classes, regions, and currencies. Stocks like Apple might have a low grade like 150 while risky penny stocks might have a risk grade of more than 500.

For individual investors, it's a good site to use to determine if the returns you are getting on the securities in your portfolio are commensurate for the risk you are taking. In short, are you getting enough reward for the risks you are taking? The site allows you to map out your holdings, including ETFs, mutual funds, stocks, and even currencies on a risk-reward matrix. You can even perform "what if" scenarios like "what if I replaced the Pfizer shares in my portfolio with Apple shares? Would my risk/reward picture improve?" For a bigger picture of the market overall, you can review their "Risk Map of the Market," to see a snapshot risk reward profile for the S&P 500.

Investor's Business Daily (www.investors.com)

This site isn't free. A subscription to eIBD will cost you $259 per year. However, if you are a fan of William O'Neil's *Investor's Business Daily* or the CAN SLIM stock selection method, or liked the invest-ment best-seller that launched his empire, *How to Make Money in Stocks*, then you should consider subscribing to IBD. This is a site for those wanting to identify hot stocks. Its IBD 100 is made up of equities that lead the market. However, there is also plenty of education on this web site to help you learn how to spot trends in stocks and identify good investment ideas. I like the Stock Check Up feature. Just punch in a ticker, and you can quickly find out how Disney, for example, measures up to its industry peers in terms of certain technicals and fundamentals like relative strength, accumulation/distribution, earnings, sales, or ROE. The site also has a handy feature that allows you to listen to the sto-ries on the web site instead of reading them. You can also create watch lists, set up alerts, and easily download any of the content you want to read when you are offline.

American Association of Individual Investors (www.aaii.com)

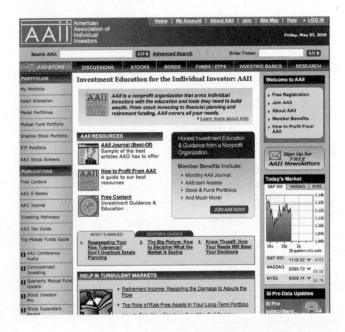

For novice and intermediate investors, there aren't many subscription memberships as valuable as AAII. This site contains content not just for making you a better investor but also for helping you with your taxes, estate planning, IRAs, and even e-broker selection. Investor education is paramount at this Chicago-based nonprofit, and members get access to all of the AAII Journals, plus a mutual fund guide and to one of my favorite areas of the site, the AAII Stock Screens. AAII stock screens offer more than 60 preset screens ranging from fundamentally focused cash-rich firms and Dogs of the Dow to others that try to emulate guru strategies from Warren Buffett's style and William Oneil's CAN SLIM to John Templeton and Peter Lynch. The site just launched some new discussion boards, which look promising. Membership costs $49 per year including its quarterly Computerized Investing newsletter and web site.

FundAlarm (www.fundalarm.com)

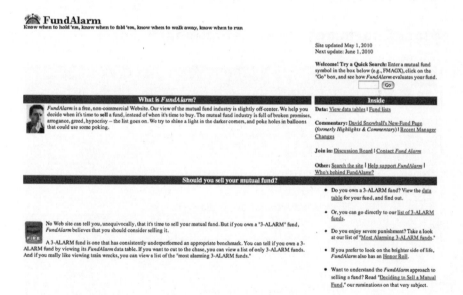

Most investing web sites trip over themselves to offer you advice about what to buy. It's often their way of getting you to click around more, building up their web site traffic, which they sell advertising against. What I like about FundAlarm is that it tells mutual fund and ETF investors which funds are bad for their portfolio health. The site was created by Roy Weitz, a California lawyer and CPA turned fund industry watchdog.

Roy has a list of so-called alarming funds that investors should stay away from or dump from their portfolios. He also has a list of honor roll funds that are okay to hold. Much of his focus is on the fees mutual funds charge. Fees and tax efficiency are about the only thing in the fund-buying business that are transparent and easily predictable. He also keeps a sharp eye on fund management and will single out misbehavior or management changes in a heartbeat.

Weitz recently called out the Congressional Effect Fund (CEFFX)[2] as the most idiotic mutual fund of the lot. Its plan is to go to cash or short-term notes whenever Congress was in session and invest in the S&P 500 when Congress is out of session. If you want to learn what to avoid, which is key to becoming a better investor, bookmark this web site and visit it regularly.

StockCharts.com (www.stockcharts.com)

Having grown up at *Forbes* under the direction of its long-time value investing–loving editor, James W. Michaels, I have a bias against technical analysis or the use of historical price and volume statistics to determine the future direction of stock prices. We were taught that reading charts was dumb. However, I can attest that some of the best advisors incorporate momentum into their strategies, and most of them do look at charts occasionally to help them make decisions.

There is some logic to this. After all, if stock prices reflect demand and supply, which in turn is affected by market psychology, then you shouldn't discount technicals. If masses of investors believe in moving averages or Fibonacci retracement levels, and make investment decisions based on them, then this is something you should pay attention to.

Some of the best Web-based charting software is available on StockCharts.com, which will allow you to map out stocks with dozens of different technical variables. There are also easy-to-use "perf charts" that let you graphically compare performance of different indexes, stocks or funds. The site's Chart School is excellent for boning up on technical analysis, and if you become a subscriber, you gain access to better charting software and more than 60 different stock scans. (Membership ranges from $14.95 to $34.90 per month.)

Other Sites to Bookmark

AlphaClone (www.alphaclone.com)

Founder Mebane Faber is a hedge fund manager who wrote a book called *The Ivy Portfolio*. It explains how the best-performing endowment funds, namely Yale and Harvard, are *not* buy-and-hold investors. He argues for smart tactical asset allocation. His Web venture, AlphaClone, offers the chance to track the holdings of top investment managers. The data comes from SEC filings, and you can easily create your own clones of these funds and back-test them going back to 2000. Or you can make custom fund-of-funds to track. One successful fund that AlphaClone features is called Tiger Cubs because it tracks the funds of money managers who used to work for Julian Robertson's Tiger Management.

Barron's (www.barrons.com)

It would be remiss for me to neglect *Barron's* in a chapter on legendary investor incubators. *Barron's* has been the bible for serious investors for many decades and continues to be an important publication. Its web site contains all of the great investing commentary of the magazine plus the ability to drill deeper into stories and financial statistics. Many of the investors profiled in this book were weaned on *Barron's*.

ETF Channel (www.etfchannel.com)

This is a new ETF-focused site worth watching in part because it was created by the same people who created ValueForum .com (described previously). ETFs are red hot among investors, and this site allows you to search and sort ETFs in a host of different ways using its ETF Finder. A key to this site is that its software allows you to drill down into the guts of exchange-traded funds. Some of the screens include the ability to find which ETFs hold stocks that are being most recommended by analysts. You can also screen by stock ticker to find out which ETFs hold the same stocks as say Berkshire Hathaway.

Forbes.com (www.forbes.com)

Okay I will admit that I am a bit biased about Forbes.com given my tenure at the media company. Some people don't realize that besides Forbes' famous lists, there is a treasure trove of excellent investing advice and insight published daily on the web site. The site's Intelligent Investing section, which features Steve Forbes video interviews with smart investors like Monhish Pabrai, Joel Greenblatt, and Jack Bogle are worth watching. And the videos aren't merely the sound bite journalism you might get on Fox or CNBC. Steve digs deep in his interviews. There is also a ton of investment commentary served up daily on Forbes .com's various sections. I am starting a blog called The Buffetts Next Door on the site where I will profile outstanding individual investors and highlight their picks.

Google Finance (www.google.com/finance)

Like Yahoo, Google is a force to be reckoned with when it comes to aggregating important financial information on companies. Each month it seems that its charting and screening software improves. Tear sheets are excellent, and what is nice is that they are not proprietary about linking off to competing sites like MSN and Yahoo.

Hedge Fund Letters (www.hedgefundletters.com)

Come here to browse the recent shareholder letters of famous money managers and hedge funds from Berkshire Hathaway to Apaloosa Management and the Sequoia Fund. The stuff may be a bit dated but there is plenty of wisdom here.

Investopedia.com (www.investopedia.com)

Use this web site as your financial dictionary on the Web. It covers everything from "basis point" to "credit default swaps" to "zero-coupon convertible notes." For novices, the tutorials are excellent like the one called "Greatest Investors," which gives you an overview of the investing styles of famous investors from Jesse Livermore and Benjamin Graham to former hedge fund star Julian Robertson.

InvestorsHub.com (www.investorshub.com)

I have not spent a lot of time on this message board–centric web site, but based on the fact that many of the Warren Buffetts Next Door use this site to generate ideas and discuss stocks, it is definitely worth bookmarking. The site is run by British firm, ADVFN, plc, which operates several other investor-oriented sites. Its no-nonsense front page acts as a quick starting point to drill deeper into discussions of active stocks. It also serves up the most active boards and presents easy tab clicks for biggest percentage gainers and losers. *Warning:* Much of the discussion on the site is about micro-cap stocks so you need to be mindful of touters and pump and dumps.

Market Folly (www.marketfolly.com)

This blog attempts to follow the smart money. By that I mean it tracks the movements of at least 40 prominent hedge funds like Seth Klarman's Baupost Group, Stephen Mandel's Lone Pine Capital, David Einhorn's Greenlight Capital, and Steven Cohen's SAC Capital. Specific investments are reported on, but they are often dated because of the SEC filing disclosure lag.

Seeking Alpha (www.seekingalpha.com)

This site is an aggregation of financial blogs, advisory and journalist content. Thousands of outside "experts" contribute to the web site daily. The site is useful for checking the pulse of the pundits and finding out what they think about the market. One problem is that there are a lot of self-promoters on the site, so please read the disclaimers and the bios of authors. They have a useful daily e-letter called *Wall Street Breakfast* that delivers pertinent market headlines of the day to your inbox. I also like the searchable full text earnings call transcripts that are posted on the site. As an investor, it's a good way to gain unfiltered access to management's ideas and plans.

Value Investor Insight (www.valueinvestorinsight.com)

This web site is the home base of a subscription newsletter (delivered electronically) that is devoted to profiling and interviewing the best professional value investors among mutual fund and hedge fund managers. It is run by former Forbes editor and senior publishing executive John Heins and his hedge fund manager partner Whitney Tilson. Each letter is packed with wisdom and stock ideas from investment mavens ranging from Warren Buffett and Bill Miller to Pershing Square's Bill Ackman. A subscription costs $350, but if you're a value investor it's well worth it.

Yahoo Finance (http://finance.yahoo.com)

The mother of all investment portals, Yahoo Finance continues to lead the pack on news and data relevant to investors. Tear sheets and interactive charts are great, and for investors, the "key stats" come in handy when quickly comparing companies.

YCharts.com (www.ycharts.com)

Every day I am amazed at the neat new tools I find on the Web. YCharts is a site designed for those that focus on fundamentals who like to see things graphically. Think valuation metrics, like revenue growth or price-earnings ratios or receivables turnover. Want to know the cash on hand at the company versus the dividend yield? A few clicks will bring up an impressive chart of the data delivered directly from SEC filings.

Zero Hedge (www.zerohedge.com)

This blog's tagline is "On a long enough timeline, the survival rate for everyone drops to zero." This is a great site for investors prone to getting caught up in market euphoria. Its contributors takes a sober (read: bearish) look at nearly all market and geopolitical events. For contrarian value investors this blog is a must-read.

Notes

Introduction

1. Marketocracy.com, as of March 31, 2010.
2. Ibid.
3. ValueForum.com. Return is calculated by investing into the first contest entry, cashing out the positions at the end of the contest, investing the proceeds into the next contest entry, and so on.

Chapter 1

1. Marketocracy.com, as of March 31, 2010.
2. Acquired by Reliance Infocom in 2004.

Chapter 2

1. ValueForum.com, based on Krebs's ValueForum quarterly stock-picking contest results. Calculated by investing into the first contest entry, cashing out the positions at the end of the contest, investing the proceeds into the next contest entry, and so on (as of March 31, 2010).
2. "Do Option Sellers Have a Trading Edge?" by John Summa, CTA, Ph.D. www.investopedia.com/articles/optioninvestor/03/100103.asp?viewed=1.
3. Investopedia.com, definitions of call and put option.
4. Barrons.com, "Pooling and Fooling," by Abraham J. Briloff, Oct. 23, 2000, http://online.barrons.com/article/SB972089231571988533.html.

Chapter 3

1. Marketocracy.com, as of March 31, 2010.
2. *Forbes*, "Seize the Day," January 7, 2008; and "Dickensian Days," February 2, 2009, both by David Dreman.
3. GuruFocus.com, "Wisdom from Seth Klarman," October 7, 2009.
4. Barrons.com, "Mortgage Lands Latest Peril: A Value Trap," by Jonathon R. Laing, September 17, 2007.

Chapter 4

1. Marketocracy.com, as of March 31, 2010.
2. Marketocracy.com. All performance data is as of March 31, 2010. Kai Petainen's Energy and Utilities Fund and Kai's Materials and Consumer Staples Fund inception dates, March 18, 2003 and March 19, 2003, respectively. Kai Petainen's diversified fund inception date February 11, 2003.
3. Investopedia.com, definition of "Super Bowl Indicator."

Chapter 5

1. ValueForum.com, as of March 31, 2010.
2. ValueForum.com. based on Hill's ValueForum quarterly stock picking contest results. Calculated by investing into the first contest entry, cashing out the positions at the end of the contest, investing the proceeds into the next contest entry, and so on (as of March 31, 2010).
3. CrunchBase.com, Companies, Cake Financial.
4. TechCrunch.com, "Cake Financial Acquired by E*Trade," by Jason Kincaid, January 14, 2010.
5. Reuters, "Former Southwestern Resources CEO Admits Fraud," June 25, 2009, reporting by Cameron French, editing by Peter Galloway.
6. Fairmark.com, "Tax Guide for Investors, Recharacterization Overview," by Kaye A. Thomas, January 24, 2008.
7. Forbes.com, "Single-Stock Retirement Plan," by Matthew Schifrin, November 14, 2006.

Chapter 6

1. Marketocracy.com, as of March 31, 2010.
2. Formerly (NASDAQ: IOMI). Company is now owned by Intercell, AG.
3. Iomai IPO Prospectus dated February 1, 2006.
4. Iomai web site, Clinical Development, www.iomai.com/content/view/13/27/.
5. Iomai Fact Sheet, June 2007 data.
6. *Washington Post*, "Merck to Test Iomai Patch for Boosting Vaccine Immunity," by Michael S. Rosenwald, www.washingtonpost.com/wp-dyn/content/article/2008/04/03/AR2008040303847.html.
7. Homeland Security Newswire (HSNW), Intercell to acquire Iomai, May 15, 2008 (http://homelandsecuritynewswire.com/intercell-acquire-iomai).

Chapter 7

1. Marketocracy.com, as of March 31, 2010.
2. In the Matter of BMO Nesbitt Burns Inc. and Thomas Waitt, Manitoba Securities Commission, Order No. 3327, May 9, 2001. www.msc.gov.mb.ca/legal_docs/orders/bmonesbitt.html.

3. St. Louis Federal Reserve, Research, "Spot Oil Price: West Texas Intermediate," http://research.stlouisfed.org/fred2/data/OILPRICE.txt.
4. *Forbes*, "The World's Billionaires 2010," www.forbes.com, #316, March 10, 2010.

Chapter 8

1. ValueForum.com quarterly contest results.
2. TSHAOnline, The Handbook of Texas Online, Oil and Gas Industry, www.tshaonline.org/handbook/online/articles/OO/doogz.html.
3. Arkansas Business.com, "Arkansas Business Hall of Fame, Frank Lyon, Sr.," www.arkansasbusiness.com/people_hall_fame.asp?id=22.
4. WRTG Economics, "Oil Price History and Analysis (Updating)," www.wtrg.com/prices.htm.
5. P. Zihlmann, "Investment Management AG, Wheaton River Minerals report" (editorial), www.gold-eagle.com/editorials_03/zihlmann100603.html.

Chapter 9

1. Marketocracy.com, as of March 31, 2010.
2. Ibid.
3. Marketocracy.com, Uyehara trading records.
4. Medivation.com—Newsroom: Medivation Presents Positive Data on Demebon's Long-Term Efficacy . . . ," July 30, 2008.

Chapter 10

1. Marketocracy.com, as of March 31, 2010.
2. Fibonacci, www.fibonacci.name/index.html.
3. Investopedia.com, "Fibonacci and the Golden Ratio," by Justin Kuepper.
4. Elliott Wave International, "What is the Elliott Wave Principle?" www.elliottwave.com/introduction/elliott_wave_principle.aspx?code=ftv&.
5. S&P 500 Index—Historical Prices, http://finance.yahoo.com.
6. Infoplease.com, "Money Market Interest Rates and Mortgage Rates, 1980–2002."

Chapter 11

1. Marketocracy Masters Fund (MOFQX) performance record has been mixed. According to Morningstar, which considers the fund mid-cap blend, it has outperformed the S&P 500 only five of the eight full years it has been tracking the fund. The fund has failed to attract significant assets. Marketocracy Capital also offers separately managed accounts based on the stock picks of several of its best virtual portfolio managers including six profiled in this book.
2. Fundalarm.com, Highlights & Commentary, January 2010.

About the Author

Matt Schifrin is vice president and investing editor for Forbes Media, LLC. After many years as an investigative reporter and editor at *Forbes*, Schifrin created *Forbes Best of the Web* magazine and web site, which reviewed thousands of sites, and later went on to build Forbes Newsletter Group. Forbes publishes and distributes more than 40 investment newsletters.

Schifrin also oversees Forbes virtual event business, Forbes iConferences, as well as the Intelligent Investing section on Forbes.com. Schifrin is responsible for investing coverage at Forbes Media including its financial columnists and various investing columns and blogs. He has been a National Magazine Award finalist and has appeared numerous times on television and radio. He frequently speaks at investment conferences.

Schifrin is a graduate of Cornell University and lives in northern New Jersey with his wife, two children, dog and cat. You can find out more about him and *The Warren Buffetts Next Door* at www.mattschifrin .com or by following him on Twitter at @schifrin.

Index